C000067820

THE FORESTS OF MINDORO

BY

MELVIN L. MERRITT

FORESTER, DIVISION OF INVESTIGATION

DEPARTMENT OF THE INTERIOR
BUREAU OF FORESTRY

BULLETIN No. 8

MAJOR GEORGE P. AHERN
DIRECTOR OF FORESTRY

MANILA
BUREAU OF PRINTING
1908

77345

In the interest of creating a more extensive selection of rare historical book reprints, we have chosen to reproduce this title even though it may possibly have occasional imperfections such as missing and blurred pages, missing text, poor pictures, markings, dark backgrounds and other reproduction issues beyond our control. Because this work is culturally important, we have made it available as a part of our commitment to protecting, preserving and promoting the world's literature. Thank you for your understanding.

ILLUSTRATIONS.

PLATES.

MAP.

LETTER OF TRANSMITTAL.

DEPARTMENT OF THE INTERIOR, BUREAU OF FORESTRY,
Manila, November 10, 1908.

SIR: I have the honor to submit herewith a manuscript, entitled "The Forests of Mindoro," by Forester Melvin L. Merritt, division of investigation, and respectfully recommend its publication as Bulletin No. 8 of the Bureau of Forestry.

Very respectfully,

GEORGE P. AHERN,
Director of Forestry.

The SECRETARY OF THE INTERIOR,
Manila, P. I.

THE FORESTS OF MINDORO.

SUMMARY.

1. On the west side of Mindoro there are broad grassy areas with scattered timber. The east and northeast sides are well wooded and contain the bulk of the merchantable forest.

2. The central mountainous portion of the island is not suited for agricultural purposes and should be retained in permanent forest.

3. The coastal plains of the island, especially on the north and east, are well adapted for agricultural purposes. The timber on these should therefore be cut and the land opened for settlement as rapidly as it is desired.

4. While there is a great complexity of tree species and a number of distinct types of forest in Mindoro, the bulk of the merchantable timber is found in the dipterocarp type of forest, most of the large trees of which belong to the botanical family Dipterocarpaceæ. These dipterocarps are uniformly tall, of large diameter, and well formed.

5. It is estimated [1] that there are at least 814,000 acres (329,425 hectares) of solid commercial forest, which are practically unbroken by clearings and contain at least 5,755,300,000 feet B. M. of merchantable timber. In addition, there are approximately 262,000 acres (106,031 hectares) of commercial forest that contain scattered clearings and noncommercial forest which will yield at least 400,000,000 feet B. M. There are also large areas of low grade forest classed as noncommercial. These contain sufficient timber for the use of the local population.

6. The most desirable portions of the forest are those lying on the lower slopes of the mountains in northeastern Mindoro. Here yields of 20,000 feet B. M. per acre are found over large areas.

INTRODUCTION.

Mindoro is one of the main timber-producing districts of the Philippines, and although it has long been credited with containing rich and extensive virgin forests, comparatively little has been known regarding their location or composition. In view of this a report has been prepared, having the following objects:

(1) To make a rough, topographic map of the island.

---

[1] This estimate has been made by reducing the actual area one-half to allow for mountain tops, hillsides, river valleys, or poorer areas, which naturally occur in any forest, and applying to this area the estimates of yields, less 20 per cent for defects. It is only for species which are merchantable at present.

(2) To locate and show upon the map the forested areas and other types of vegetation.

(3) To determine roughly the composition of commercially forested areas.

(4) To offer practical suggestions for lumbering operations.

The Coast and Geodetic Survey charts furnish the basis for the map constructed. Use has also been made of various sketches and maps secured from the Bureau of Lands, from the Military Information Division, and from other sources. This material has been supplemented by a large number of original notes taken by the author. So far as possible, errors regarding geographic names have been corrected. In cases where any name given on the Coast and Geodetic charts has been changed, the old one is added with the letters "C. & G. S." written beneath.

Botanical collections made by the writer and deposited with the Bureau of Science serve as a basis for the botanical nomenclature of this report.

GENERAL DESCRIPTION OF MINDORO.

SITUATION AND AREA.

The Island of Mindoro is situated about 100 miles (161 kilometers) southwest of Manila, just west of the southern portion of Luzon. It extends from 120° 17′ to 121° 33′ east longitude and from 12° 13′ to 13° 31′ north latitude. It is the seventh island of the Archipelago in size, containing an area of 3,851 square miles. Several adjacent islands, relatively unimportant from a forest point of view, have also been included in the map.

TOPOGRAPHY.

Extending the entire length of the island, from northwest to southeast, is a broad range of mountains (Pl. II), which at its highest point, Mount Halcon, in the north central part reaches an elevation of about 2,590 meters (8,500 feet). Lower spurs from this main range extend eastward toward Pinamalayan and Sumagui and westward to the vicinity of Santa Cruz (Pl. III, fig. 1) and between Iriron and Sablayan. Lower isolated mountain areas are found on the east side of the island north of Pinamalayan and east of Lake Naujan. A low pass between Mamburao and Abra de Ilog cuts the Mount Calavite range from the main central chain, forming a separate mountain mass in the northwest part of the Island.

On either side of the main mountain system lower foothills extend to the broad alluvial coastal plains. (Pl. III, fig. 2.) These, varying in width from 1 to 15 miles, are usually nearly flat, and slope very gradually from the beach to the foothills where they have an altitude of from 200 to 400 feet.

Many of the smaller islands adjacent to Mindoro are made up of low

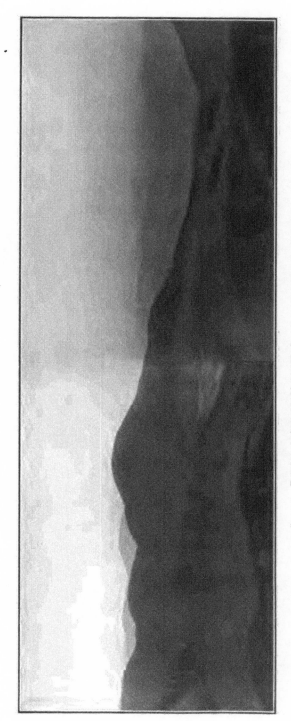

PLATE II. TYPICAL COGON GRASS COVERED HILLS OF WESTERN MINDORO.

(Southwest of Mount Halcon ; about 3,000 feet above sea level.)

FIG. 1. LOW PARANG SOUTHEAST OF SANTA CRUZ.

(Note pine trees along top of ridge. Acleng parang (*Albizzia* sp.) left foreground.
Antidesma sp. right foreground.)

FIG. 2. TYPICAL PARANG.

(Looking across valley of Mompong River from the west.)

PLATE III.

limestone hills. Ilin is one of the largest of these and is most important from a forest point of view. A few of the smaller ones are mere sand banks.

CLIMATE.

The moist winds of the northeast monsoon, which come at the normal dry season, from November to May, pass over the low portion of Luzon to the east, thence over the Verde Island Passage, and reach Mindoro with a considerable amount of moisture still retained in the air. Owing to the presence of high mountains in the center of the island practically all of this moisture falls on the north and east sides, giving to those sections a considerable rainfall during the driest season, while but a small amount is noted on the west coast at this period of the year. During the other monsoon, the southwest winds strike directly on the western coast of Mindoro and much of the moisture carried by them is precipitated before passing over the high range in the center of the island, hence the rainfall on the east coast at this time of the year is considerably less than on the west. Thus it happens that western Mindoro has a very marked wet and dry season, while upon the east coast the rainfall is much more evenly distributed throughout the year. The following table, taken from the reports of the Weather Bureau, although very incomplete, illustrates the point:

Monthly rainfall, in millimeters, at Pinamalayan and Mamburao, Mindoro.

Month.	Pinamalayan.			Mamburao.				
	1907.	1908.	Mean.	1896.	1897.	1898.	1899.	Mean.
January	73.4	128.3	100.8			5.3	1	3.2
February	73.4	35	54.2				2.3	2.3
March	24.6	57.7	41.1				9.4	9.4
April	32	47.2	39.6		29.9			29.9
May	68.8	142.7	105.7		86.5	457		271.8
June	86.9		86.9		367.7	822.2		595
July	86.9		86.9		426.4	229.5		327
August	207		207		698.6	1,295.5		997
September	69.9		69.9		497.6	473.2		485.4
October	218.6		213.6	254.7	391.8			323.2
November	117.1		117.1	18.2	78.2			48.2
December	421.1		421.1	7.4	39.9			23.6
Annual	1,474.7		ª1,543.9					ᵇ3,116

ª 60.7 inches.   ᵇ 122.5 inches.

ROADS AND TRAILS.

A road from Calapan to Naujan is the only one of any length passable for wheeled vehicles. Many of the main towns are connected by horse trails, while footpaths are usually found in the forests, and are very common throughout the cultivated sections of the country. None of these trails would be useful in carrying on logging operations, although some of them might serve for the transportation of supplies to parties operating in the forest. The nature of the soil is such, however, that good logging roads can be made in almost all of the less hilly and the more level portions of the island.

RIVERS.

Although the rivers of Mindoro are usually short, yet they are fairly broad, and have rapid currents. (Pl. IV.) During the rainy season the main streams have a width of from 50 to 300 meters and a depth of 1 meter or more. Freshets increase this size, while dry weather reduces it greatly. While many of the larger rivers might be used for floating timber from the forest, it is believed that large lumbering concerns will find it much more satisfactory to depend upon logging railroads for this purpose. The Baco and Lumanbayan Rivers, however, are sufficiently large and deep to serve during all but the driest seasons. All of the rivers, except the Caguray, have sand bars at their mouths, with depths of water at low tide usually not exceeding one meter and often less than that. High tide will add about another meter to this depth. The Caguray River, sheltered by Ilin Island, has no pronounced sand bar, and is about 2 meters deep at its mouth.

SOCIAL AND ECONOMIC CONDITIONS.

Mindoro, with its adjacent islands, supports a population of 47,465. Of these, 40,197[1] are of the civilized races, and 7,268[2] of the wild tribes.

The Christian Filipinos, composed principally of Tagalogs and Visayans, occupy the land in and adjacent to the coast towns. They live mainly by agriculture or fishing, and by the various forest industries. They draw on the forest for timber to build houses and boats, for firewood, bejuco (rattan), and other forest products. These demands may be easily met without causing any serious drain upon forest resources.

The wild tribes, or Mangyans, as they are called, are a timid people, living usually in the hills or central mountains. They practice a rude system of agriculture, making their clearings in different places from year to year, thus inflicting much damage upon the forest. (Pl. V., figs. 1 and 2.) In the mountain region west of Bongabon and north from Bulalacao, where these people are now most numerous, they have destroyed practically all the merchantable forest.

OWNERSHIP OF THE LAND.

The main part of the grass areas of the east and northeast coast, and those portions near to the settlements in other places, as well as land actually under cultivation, are claimed as private land. Much of this is held under some kind of unperfected title or merely by right of possession. A great deal of it is in comparatively small holdings,

[1] Data secured from the 1908 census of Mindoro taken by Capt. L. J. Van Schaick, governor of Mindoro.

[2] Figures taken from the 1903 census of the Philippine Islands.

although on the west and southwest coast there are a number of large estates, including the San Jose friar estate, recently purchased by the Insular Government. With the exception of a few small claims, the only tract of private forest is one of 919 hectares found east of the Camarong River on the north coast of Mindoro. The rest of the land is the property of the Philippine Government, and that portion of it which is covered with forest is defined as public forest, and, as such, is under the direction and management of the Bureau of Forestry.

TYPES OF VEGETATION.

GENERAL.

Four main divisions of vegetation have been distinguished and indicated upon the map, as follows: Commercial forest, noncommercial forest, grass lands, and cultivated areas. A "commercial forest," as the term is used in this report, is one which is of a sufficiently good grade to support continued lumbering operations, while "noncommercial forests" are those of inferior grade, not suitable for lumbering.

The forest classed as noncommercial may contain many merchantable trees, often sufficient for the local population, or even for the timber cutting of small operators. "Grass lands" are those occupied principally by grass with a few scattering trees or patches of timber. "Cultivated areas" are those used in agricultural pursuits, excluding grazing. Naturally these divisions grade into each other, and in some cases, it is largely a matter of opinion how to class a given area.

The following is the estimated area which each division constitutes of the total area of the Island of Mindoro:

Class.	Hectares.	Acres.	Per cent.
Commercial forest	435, 476	1, 076, 126	44
Noncommercial forest	188, 047	464, 691	19
Grass lands	356, 298	880, 466	36
Cultivated areas	9, 896	24, 457	01
Total	989, 717	a 2, 445, 740	100

a This total is that of the entire Island of Mindoro less the area of Lake Naujan.

COMMERCIAL FOREST.

Four characteristic types of commercial forest have been distinguished, as follows: Valley and coastal plains type, dipterocarp type, dry-hill type, and mangrove-swamp type.

The valley and coastal plain forests occupy the alluvial coastal plains, the river valleys, and limited portions of the lower hills, where conditions approximate those of the first-named situations. The dipterocarp forests are found on the hill and mountain slopes and the lower portions where there is a deep, rich soil, good drainage, and an abundance of water.

The dry-hill forests occupy the lower mountain and hill regions, preferably those of a limestone formation, usually in places having a pronounced dry soil. The mangrove forests grow upon the broad tidal flats situated near the mouths of the larger rivers. These are normally flooded at high tide.

VALLEY AND COASTAL PLAINS TYPE.

This type of forest is characterized by a great complexity of tree species, comparatively few of which are at present commercially valuable, and a great majority of which do not reach a merchantable size. It presents a dense tangled appearance, in which are scattered large trees, with many smaller ones crowded together beneath them forming an under story. Over and through this tree growth a mass of vines and bejucos (rattan) runs in profusion. On the ground shrubs, herbs, and the seedling stages of the larger growing plants are numerous.

Although the composition of the forests of this type differs considerably according to the situation, the following trees are the most constant and important of the larger kinds: White Lauan (*Pentacme contorta*), Narra (*Pterocarpus indicus*) (frontispiece), Apitong (*Dipterocarpus* spp.), Malugay (*Pometia pinnata*), Ipil (*Intsia acuminata* and *I. bijuga*), Guijo (*Shorea guiso*), Amuguis (*Koordersiodendron pinnatum*), Calumpit, Sacat, etc. (*Terminalia* spp.), Bolongeta (*Diospyros pilosanthera*), Dao (*Dracontomelum dao*), Malaicmo (*Celtis philippinensis*), Candol-candol (*Sterculia blancoi*), and Toog (*Bischofia trifoliata*). All but the last four named of these species are of recognized commercial value.

It will be noticed by this list as well as by Tables I to V, in Appendix A, that the members of the botanical family Dipterocarpeæ (Lauan, Apitong, Hagachac, and Guijo) occupy a prominent place in the forest and comprise a large part of the merchantable yield. The presence of a large number of other trees, however, gives a distinctly different character to the forest from that of the hill regions where dipterocarps reach their best development, and warrant the distinguishing of this forest as a type. It might well have been called "valley and coastal plain dipterocarp forest."

In the under story is a great complexity of species, of which Butong Manok (*Cyclostemon* sp.), several species each of the genera *Canarium, Eugenia,* and *Palaquium,* and of the botanical family Myristicaceæ are among the most common. Putat (*Barringtonia* sp.) and Catmon (*Dillenia philippinensis*) are common in the moister places.

On the lower mountain slopes, along stream banks, and in other places where there is good drainage and abundant water supply, the forest often forms an entirely closed crown, thus crowding out much of

Fig. 1. MANGYAN SHACK.

(Used by them for three or four months while making and planting clearing for rice.)

Fig. 2. TYPICAL "CAIÑGIN" OR CLEARING IN FOREST.

(North of Alag River.)

PLATE V.

the undergrowth. Here Malugay is the most common tree, and in hill regions especially, gives character to the forest, forming what might be classed as a distinct type. In poorly drained situations large trees are more scattered and the undergrowth is very dense. In extremely dry places much of this undergrowth is replaced by climbing bamboo which grows over and under the trees or falls down on the ground, forming almost impenetrable thickets. Palms [1] are very common in favorable places in this type of forest.

The soil of the coastal plain is a fine, deep, alluvial deposit, compact, not well nor easily drained. Although a thin layer at the surface is usually mixed with humus and is much more friable than the rest, the amount of leaf mold and litter is small. On the slopes the soil is more mixed with gravel or stone, and is much more open and better drained.

Most of the tree species seed abundantly, but the dense shade usually found prevents the best growth of seedlings, or kills them out entirely. Seedlings of noncommercial species greatly outnumber those of desirable kinds, even where conditions for reproduction are most favorable. In places, however, where the undergrowth is not too dense, reproduction is usually sufficient to maintain the present stand.

The merchantable condition of the forest is poor. Not only are many of the trees defective or stunted, but this forest, located as it is in the most accessible places, has long been subject to culling and clearing by the coast inhabitants, hence it has lost many of its best trees.

A good idea of the stands and yields, which vary greatly, depending upon the conditions in which the forests grow, may be obtained from Tables I to V, in Appendix A.

It is estimated that there are approximately 174,000 acres (about 70,400 hectares) of this type of forest which is practically unbroken by clearings or by noncommercial forest. Reducing the area one-half, to allow for openings or poorer grade areas which occur in any forest, and applying to the result the average yield of the areas estimated, less 20 per cent for defects, or 7,800 feet B. M. per acre, there is a total yield of 678,600,000 feet B. M.

Under present market conditions this type of forest does not offer the best inducements to the large timber operator, since so much heavier and denser stands may be obtained in the dipterocarp type of forest. For the small lumberman, however, using the primitive method of logging generally employed, this type is the most desirable, for it lies closest to the shore and contains a sufficient amount of timber to meet his demands.

[1] For a statement of the stand of palms, see Merritt and Whitford; A Preliminary Working Plan for the Public Forest Tract of the Mindoro Lumber and Logging Company, Bureau of Forestry, P. I., Bulletin 6, p. 16.

DIPTEROCARP TYPE.

The most important type of forest is that growing upon the hill and mountain slopes and on the lower mountains. Although the larger part of it lies northeast of the main central range where moisture is abundant and soil and drainage are such as to form the most favorable conditions for forest growth, it is probable that large areas, now occupied mainly by grass, were at one time covered with a dipterocarp type of forest. A fragment of such a forest was noted on a north slope, south of the Pagbahan River, at a distance of 16 kilometers from the beach. Here a count on 2.41 hectares (5.95 acres) showed 42.3 Apitong (*Dipterocarpus grandiflorus*) trees, the predominant species, per hectare, and an estimated yield of 11,800 feet B. M. per acre.

Upon the higher mountains the forest becomes much poorer, the best grades seldom reaching greater altitudes than about 600 to 760 meters (2,000 to 2,500 feet). It is characterized by a less dense undergrowth than other types of forest and by heavy stands of large and tall-growing species (Pl. VI), making it a closed forest, nearly all of the trees of which belong to the botanical family Dipterocarpaceæ, hence the term "dipterocarp forest." It must be remembered, however, that dipterocarps are by no means confined to this forest, but that certain species occur in almost all types except the mangrove swamps. The main species, commercially and numerically, are Tanguile (*Shorea polysperma*), Alam, or Red Lauan (*Shorea squamata*), Apitong (*Dipterocarpus* spp.), White Lauan (*Pentacme contorta*), Palosapis (*Anisoptera thurifera*), and Yacal (*Hopea* spp.). (Pl. VII, Figs. 1 and 2.)

These dipterocarps usually occur well mixed throughout the forest. Tanguile is most numerous on moist ridges and slopes above 210 meters (about 700 feet) altitude, where it sometimes forms nearly pure stands. Alam, or Red Lauan, grows best on the lower hill slopes where it is by far the commonest tree. Apitong proper seeks the drier ridges and slopes, while Panao occurs more generally at lower elevations and in moister situations. Yacal occurs in small quantities only.

Tanguile is the largest of these trees, and reaches a diameter of 150 centimeters (59 inches) or more, and a clear length of from 20 to 35 meters (65 to 115 feet). The other species approximate this size, Alam, or Red Lauan, being the shortest, with clean boles seldom reaching more than 20 to 25 meters (65 to 82 feet) in clear length.

Without question, it will be to these species and to this type of forest that the islands must look for the main future supply of timber.

Growing under these large trees are numerous smaller kinds. These, however, do not occur so thickly as in the previous type. *Canarium minutiflorum*, Palo Maria (*Calophyllum* spp.), Baticulin (*Phoebe sterculioides*), Basan (*Garcinia eugeniaefolia*), *Palaquium* spp., and numerous members of the botanical families Meliaceæ and Myristicaceæ are the most noticeable in this growth.

PLATE VI. INTERIOR VIEW OF FOREST SHOWING GOOD STAND OF DIPTEROCARPS.
(Between Binabay and Alag Rivers. Trees from 2 to 4 feet in diameter.)

Fig. 2. VIEW IN OUTER PORTION OF DIPTEROCARP FOREST.

Plate VII—Continued.

Vines, bejuco (rattan), and very small trees are still common, though much less noticeably so than in the previous types. Often the forest contains so little undergrowth that one may travel through it without much inconvenience.

The soil is usually moist, rich, fairly deep, and well drained, and although stones and rock outcrops are not uncommon, the conditions are well suited for tree growth. Here, as elsewhere, litter and leaf mold is scanty.

The topography varies with the situation, but in areas where these forests are best developed, as in the foothill region northeast of the central high mountain chain, the country is usually made up of long gradual slopes and ridges. The higher, steeper mountains and mountain sides are less heavily wooded.

The dipterocarps seed plentifully during seed years. These occur at frequent intervals, the exact length of which is not known. After a good seed year the ground under the trees is covered with seed which usually sprout readily. The seedlings, however, are very tender, not doing well either in full shade or places too open. Many of them die a short time after sprouting, if exposed to too much light. Once started, however, they are of vigorous growth and hold their own in the forest. Saplings and small poles are usually sufficiently abundant to guarantee future crops. By taking ordinary care of this young growth in logging and by retaining seed trees of desirable kinds, the reproduction of the forest will be assured in any ordinary situation.

Tables VI to VIII, in Appendix A, will give some idea of the stand and yield of this type of forest.

It is estimated that there are approximately 502,000 acres (about 203,000 hectares) of this type of forest unbroken by clearings or by noncommercial forest areas. This contains an estimated yield of 17,900 feet B. M. per acre, or a total of 4,492,900,000 feet B. M.[1]

As already stated, this type offers good opportunity for extensive lumbering operations, due to the large areas, the heavy stands, the long, clean form of the principal trees, and proximity to the seashore.

The choicest portion of this forest lies in the northwestern part of the Island, between the Subaan (San Teodoro) and the Pula Rivers. Of this portion, the part southwest of Lake Naujan and that between the Alag and the Subaan Rivers, is most accessible. From this forest timber may be taken directly to Lake Naujan, which is deep and navigable throughout, thence down the Laguna River to the beach or to a sawmill, an excellent location for which is found at the junction of the San Agustin and the Laguna Rivers. The river from the lake to this point is always deep and navigable, while the part from there to the

---

[1] Area and yield calculated as for valley type (see p. 15).

beach is quite shallow during the dry season. The area southwest of the lake is made up of ridges running back from the lake and varies in altitude from 100 to 800 feet, so that few engineering difficulties would be encountered in laying out logging roads. Between the Alag and the Subaan Rivers long ridges with short side spurs extend west toward the mountains. These reach an altitude of 400 meters (about 1,300 feet) 10 kilometers (about 6 miles) inland.

The mouth of the Baco River is sufficiently deep for the entrance of barges or small steamers. A mill located upon its banks just below Chicago would draw upon the above-mentioned area and upon the forest tributary to the southern branches of the Alag and around the head of the Catuiran River. This site has sufficient land upon which to place a mill, abundant fresh water, and can be easily connected by telephone with the telegraph station at Calapan.

DRY-HILL TYPE.

This type of forest grows in low mountainous regions upon thin, rocky soils, usually those of a limestone formation. Molave (*Vitex littoralis* and *V. pubescens*) and Duñgon (*Tarrietia sylvatica*) are quite characteristic of the type and seldom occur outside of it. Molave, which is botanically related to the well-known teak wood, has a low-spreading habit of growth usually not exceeding 6 or 8 meters (about 20 to 25 feet) in merchantable length and 100 centimeters (39 inches) in diameter when mature. It is found near the seacoast in open places. From five to seven trees per hectare (about 2 to 3 per acre), over small areas only, would be about its maximum stand.

Duñgon, while growing well in places similar to those occupied by Molave, is more tolerant and occurs as well in heavier forests. It is a tall tree, reaching a merchantable height of 25 meters (82 feet) and a diameter of 120 centimeters (47 inches) in exceptional cases.

Other widely distributed trees, characteristic of this type, are Calantas (*Toona calantas*), Camagon (*Diospyros discolor*), Bigaa (*Zizyphus mollis*), Alacaac (*Palaquium oleiferum*), and Manicnic (*Palaquium* spp.).

Calantas, the tree which yields the soft cedar-like wood valuable for making cigar boxes, has often been reported as abundant throughout many parts of Mindoro. As a matter of fact it is nowhere common on the island and, although widely distributed in moist situations in this and to some extent in other types, it is doubtful if for any considerable area the stand, even in the best places, is one tree to the hectare.

Narra (*Pterocarpus indicus*) and Liusin (*Parinarium griffithianum*) are quite numerous on many of the lower and more open hills and valleys bordering this type of forest.

Ebony (*Maba buxifolia*) occurs scattered over the low dry hills in the Amnay River basin and in a few other favorable places, and although

Fig. 1. TYPICAL THICKET OF CLIMBING BAMBOO.

(West of Abra de Ilog. Large tree in background is Tanguile (*Shorea polysperma*).)

PLATE VIII.

FIG. 2. INTERIOR VIEW OF DRY HILLS FOREST.

(South of Bulalacao.)

PLATE VIII—Continued.

hardly of commercial importance, it is interesting on account of the valuable wood produced. The Ebony trees noted seldom exceeded 30 centimeters in diameter and have a jet-black heartwood of from one-half to one-fourth of their diameter.

Between and under the large trees are herbs, shrubs, small trees, and numerous vines. Very often on dry slopes and ridges, climbing bamboo forms dense thickets which crowd out the larger portion of other small growth. (Pl. VIII, figs. 1 and 2.)

In places where conditions approximate those of the river-valley type of forest, the growth becomes more dense and the composition of the two types grade together. Such is the case with the forests of north-western Mindoro, estimates of the stands of which are given later.

The soil is ordinarily dry and stony, although generally mixed with a considerable amount of finer material. Leaf mold, or litter, is present in small quantities only.

Although Molave seeds abundantly, most of the seedlings are killed by drought or from competition with other trees, while Dungon reproduces only slightly better. Unless, therefore, some special attention is given to improving the sylvicultural conditions of the forest, only a scattered stand of these two trees will be secured.

The merchantable and sylvicultural conditions of the forest are poor, owing to the fact that the forest has long since been culled of its most valuable trees.

Tables IX to XVII, in Appendix A, show the stand in the region about Mount Calavite in northwestern Mindoro. Here, as already stated, the forest grades into that of the valley type.

It is estimated that there are approximately 139,000 acres (about 56,200 hectares) of this type of forest which is practically unbroken by clearings or noncommercial areas. This contains an estimated yield of 8,400 feet B. M. per acre, or a total of 583,800,000 feet B. M.[1]

As a logging proposition this forest has little to offer to those desiring to work upon a large scale. Not only is the area limited, but the merchantable trees are few in number and badly scattered. To the small cutter, however, who does not require a large supply, the proposition is a good one, and with proper management it should continue to be so permanently. Molave, Dungon, Ipil, Narra, Calantas, and many other woods which find a ready sale upon the market at the highest prices, can here be secured.

MANGROVE-SWAMP TYPE.

. At the mouths of many of the larger streams and rivers are broad flat areas of delta formation, which are usually flooded at high tide. The presence of salt water in these places precludes the growth of ordinary trees and an entirely distinct type of forest has been developed.

---

[1] Area and yield calculated as for valley type (see p. 15).

Bacauan (*Rhizophora mucronata* and *R. conjugata*), Busiin (*Bruguiera gymnorrhiza*), Pototan (*Bruguiera caryophylloides* and *B. eriopetala*), and Tangal (*Ceriops roxburghiana*), all belonging to the botanical family Rhizophoraceæ, with Api-api (*Avicennia officinalis*) and Pagatpat (*Sonneratia pagatpat*), compose the forest. Where the swamps have not been cut over, the members of the family Rhizophoraceæ grow in almost pure stands, but in places they have been exploited steadily for years, and have often been replaced by the worthless Api-api. As ordinarily found, a good mangrove swamp contains from 500 to 1,000 trees per hectare, ranging in size from 10 to 30 centimeters (4 to 12 inches) in diameter and from 6 to 14 meters (20 to 45 feet) in height.

Almost invariably it was noted that the trees belonging to the genus *Rhizophora*, which are the long, prop-rooted kinds, occupy a fairly well-defined belt along the water channels and on the lower tide levels. They are the first trees to seed upon and occupy newly formed mud flats. Young trees of *Rhizophora* have been seen growing upon such land which is bare only at the lowest tides. Upon slightly higher ground, trees of the genus *Bruguiera* form nearly pure stands, finding their natural habitat where the level is approximately that of the highest tides. (Pl. IX.) Along the lines where these two conditions meet, the genera intermingle freely. In heavy stands there is little undergrowth. Reproduction is prolific where the shade from the trees is not so great as to prevent germination and growth. A reasonable amount of care to leave seed trees will ordinarily be all that is necessary to insure a continued crop.

Near the upper limits of high tide are scattering trees of various other species. Among these, *Xylocarpus obovatus* (Tabigue or Nigue), a dyebark tree, *Heritiera littoralis* (Duñgon-late), and *Aegiceras corniculatum* (Tondoc) are the commonest. *Sonneratia pagatpat* (Pagatpat) grows in many places throughout the swamp. Several other trees naturally adapted to the high lands mix with the mangrove trees along the edges of the swamps.

On open portions of the swamp bordering on tide-water streams, the Nipa palm (*Nipa fruticans*) is found. In limited areas south of the barrios of Baco and Baruyan and on a large tract on the east side of the Baruyan River, south of Caluagan Lake, Nipa has been planted. Probably nearly all of the swamp would grow Nipa, were the land not already occupied by trees.

The following estimates of the stand on the swamps of the Baco and Baruyan Rivers were made by counting the trees upon plots 100 meters long and 10 meters wide. Thirty such plots were taken in regular order throughout the swamp. Following is a summary of results obtained:

PLATE IX. INTERIOR OF A MANGROVE SWAMP.

(South of Bongabon River. Note reproduction under trees.)

Stand of trees over 10 centimeters (4 inches) in diameter, in mangrove swamps of Baco and Baruyan Rivers.

[Average of 3 hectares (7.4 acres).]

Species.	Per hectare.	Per acre.
Bruguiera spp	701	284
Rhizophora spp	136	55
Xylocarpus obovatus	42	17
Others	28	11
Total	907	367

The following list[1] shows the percentage of tannin and of extract in the bark of the principal mangrove species:

Species.	Number of analyses.	Per cent of dry weight.	
		Total extract.	Tannin.
Ceriops candolleana	3	29	19.6
Rhizophora mucronata	2	34.3	19.7
Rhizophora conjugata	5	28.9	18.6
Bruguiera gymnorrhiza	3	28.8	17.7
Bruguiera eriopetala	5	25.8	16.8
Bruguiera parviflora	4	20.1	11.6

NONCOMMERCIAL FORESTS.

If undisturbed, it is probable that nearly all of the forests of Mindoro would naturally develop into commercial grades. Exceptions, however, occur on the crest lines and upper slopes of the higher mountains where the thin soil and strong winds have caused a small stunted tree growth and on the newly made alluvial flats which lie above the tide water level. The latter condition, however, can not be regarded as permanent, being merely a stage in the natural development of the forest.

In almost any other situation commercial forests will develop, if left undisturbed. The influence of man, however, has made much of the commercial forest noncommercial. Over large areas clearings for agricultural purposes have been made and the land subsequently abandoned. These, thereupon, grow up with small rapid-growing noncommercial species, forming a second growth known locally as "calaanan," which though not permanently noncommercial, is practically so, as the clearing process is usually repeated before sufficient time elapses to produce a second crop. These calaanan areas are by far the most common on the north and east coasts where the abundant and well distributed rainfall fosters rapid tree growth.

---

[1] Analyses by Bureau of Science.

On the west coast, with its more pronounced dry seasons and consequent fires, the forests on partial clearings and areas cut over in lumbering do not so readily reproduce themselves, hence much of the forest there has been rendered noncommercial or barely of commercial grade.

Southwest of the high mountain chain stretching north and south from Mount Halcon is an area with a temperature considerably lower than that of sea level and with a well-drained and often extremely dry soil. Here conditions are right for the growth of pine (*Pinus merkusii*). This tree grows in pure stands and is found in open scattered groves along the higher ridges and slopes, sometimes extending well down toward sea level. (Pl. III, fig. 1.) This pine was observed at elevations as low as 60 meters (about 200 feet) in the vicinity of Santa Cruz, the southern part of its range, while at its northern limits it was nowhere seen below 900 meters (about 3,000 feet). Ground fires annually burning over the grass which has crept in among these trees prevent the best of reproduction and keep the forest open. A few other tree species occupy the bottoms of moist runs and stream valleys.

The highest exposed mountain ridges are usually wooded with a dense growth of small stunted trees and shrubs, over and upon which is a mass of moss, orchids, and ferns. Species of *Podocarpus, Dacrydium, Drimys, Vaccinnium,* and *Rhododendron* are the common trees in these places. Almaciga (*Agathis philippinensis*), commercially important because it produces a valuable resin, grows upon high ridges and slopes in this kind of forest. Lower down on the moister slopes, and mixed with the commercial forest belt, oaks (*Quercus* spp.) occur.

In the southern and western parts of Mindoro the broad grass areas are burned over periodically during the dry season, and only scattered trees of species able to withstand the effect of these fires, grow upon them. The commonest of these trees are Acleng parang (*Albizzia* sp.), Mambog (*Mitragyne diversifolia*), *Grewia tilaefolia,* and several species of *Antidesma.* This type of forest is known locally as "parang." Pl. III, fig. 2.) A large part of the grass land shown on the west coast of Mindoro is really of this type. Usually the trees are very scattering and of little or no value. Sometimes, however, they are very numerous. Table XIX, in Appendix A, will give some idea of the composition.

On limited areas along the flood plains of some of the larger rivers, most noticeably along the Lumintao and Bugsanga Rivers, Agoho (*Casuarina equisetifolia*), small in size, grows in pure stands. One hundred and twenty-six trees were counted on an area of one-half acre by the Lumintao River, near the sitio Gutad. This is a young stand of pure Agoho, in which the total average height of the trees is estimated at 6 meters (20 feet) and the average diameter at 9 centimeters (3.5 inches).

The future of all the noncommercial forests, with the exception of the permanent types first noted, is dependent upon circumstance. If at any time the destructive forces working upon the forest are checked, there is little doubt but that most of the area would eventually become commercially valuable. Especially is this true in the places where seed trees of commercial species are present. In the case of those areas on the northern coast, where the land is level and the soil rich and suited for agricultural purposes, such a change can not be expected, for it is probable that the future development of agriculture in this region will result in the use for that purpose of almost all of the lowland forest land.

GRASS LANDS.

It is entirely probable that all the grass area of Mindoro was at one time covered with a forest growth. This must certainly have been true in the eastern part where the process of cogon grass entering the clearings and ultimately replacing the trees may now be seen. On the west coast such a process is also taking place along the limits of the forest, while over the main body of the grassy areas the occurrence of scattered clumps of cultivated varieties of bamboo, of occasional betel-nut palms, and of small isolated forest areas, all point to the fact that an original growth has been cleared off.

Cogon grass (*Imperata exaltata* Brongn.) is the commonest species, occurring in almost all situations. (Pl. II.) So common is it, that grass lands are termed "cogonales." Along the broad stream beds where heavy washing prevents the growth of other grass, talahib (*Saccharum spontaneum* Retz.) makes its appearance, growing in thick matted clumps and forming almost impenetrable masses. (Pl. IV.) On many of the higher, drier ridges another grass, *Themeda gigantea* Hack., is the commonest one present.

Wild carabao, tamarao, wild cattle, deer, and hogs, roam over these lands. In a few places where herds of cattle are pastured, some of the grasses have proven to be well adapted for grazing purposes.

CULTIVATED LANDS.

While the land actually under cultivation comprises approximately only 1 per cent of the entire area, yet the methods of agriculture employed are highly important in their effect upon the forest, for more than one-half of the island has been reduced from a forested condition to grass lands or noncommercial forests. These remarks do not apply to the coast people who raise such permanent crops as hemp and coconuts, but do apply to the Mangyans and other irresponsible people who make clearings in the forest, plant them to rice, sweet potatoes, or some other temporary crops, and then abandon these clearings for others, after two or three years. (Pl. V.)

On the moist eastern and northern sides of the island this practice has had the least evil effects, as clearings are quickly replaced with a second growth which is again cleared after five or six years, so that usually the cleared land is rotated within a comparatively limited area. To the west, however, second growth is not so rapid and quickly becomes much mixed with cogon grass, thus permitting the entrance of fires.

INJURIES TO WHICH THE FORESTS ARE SUBJECT.

Because of continuous heat and moisture organic agencies are much more destructive in the tropics than in temperate regions. When a tree is wounded it is at once subject to attack of some kind. This is very noticeable with dipterocarps, many of which are likely to have rotten or hollow boles. Thus it is that, although trees are of rapid growth, they seldom live to be as old or produce as heavy stands of sound timber as in temperate regions.

Wind damages the forest in exposed places or during exceptionally severe storms. It leaves a wounded forest which is at once exposed to the attack of fungi. The young trees, injured principally by fallen limbs from the older trees, are thus opened to infection. Injuries are also caused by bark insects. Vines tightly wound around young trees no doubt shorten their lives. Insects, mainly borers, and fungi work much injury to fallen timber, hence logs should not be left in the forest for any considerable time after felling.

Taking conditions as they actually exist, the greater percentage of damage is due to artificial causes. As already stated, clearings made in the forest have been by far the most destructive force at work. Fires following up the clearings into which grass has entered do great damage, especially to the reproduction. While a careful patrol would no doubt prevent the largest part of this damage, the expenses would be almost prohibitive under present conditions.

In some places the forest clearings have worked serious injury by allowing the washing away of soils on steep hillsides to such an extent that reforestation would be very difficult.

For the present it is deemed impracticable to attempt measures to prevent these injuries other than ordinary precautions to guard against waste in logging and injury to the young growth.

UTILIZATION OF FOREST PRODUCTS.

GENERAL.

Timber, firewood, bejuco (rattan), tanbarks, dyebarks, gums and resins, and various other products of lesser importance, have for a long time been gathered from the forests of Mindoro.

Table XIX, in Appendix A, gives the quantity of the principal products which have been taken from these forests during the last few years, as determined by the amount of taxes collected during that period. In addition to this, there has been gathered, free of charge, a considerable quantity of forest products for personal use of the inhabitants.

LUMBERING OPERATIONS.

Those desiring to cut timber or gather other forest products are granted licenses for definite areas. Such licenses are ordinarily made out for one year, although concessions for longer periods are made to parties making investments of considerable capital in permanent enterprises. One twenty-year license agreement has already been granted for the forest area between the Uasig and the Sucol Rivers. This agreement grants a company the exclusive right to cut timber upon this tract.

Present methods of logging throughout the island are crude and inefficient. The trees are felled and cut into the desired length, and then hewed square by hand. During recent years this squaring of timber is being abandoned and many round logs are now sold.

Logging and skidding by means of carabao, which is the method commonly used, is especially unsatisfactory. Not only is it comparatively expensive and exceedingly slow, but the lack of animals and forage, as well as the great weight of Philippine timbers, will effectually prevent the development of large logging operations by this system. Steam logging and skidding machinery in the woods, with a logging railroad to the point of shipment, will no doubt prove to be the most satisfactory equipment.

Filipino labor is employed almost entirely and when properly managed is very satisfactory. Wages range from ₱0.50[1] to ₱1.50 per day. Usually labor can not be secured locally but must be brought in from the main centers of population. Once settled, laborers' take readily to the work and are easily satisfied.

The principal timber species cut in Mindoro are: Guijo, Narra, Molave, Calantas, Ipil, Duñgon, Apitong, Lauan, Malugay, Amuguis, and Acleng parang. Many of these come from areas comparatively close to the coast—these areas only being available under present methods. A few logs of Tanguile and Mayapis are cut for bancas (native boats) in northeastern Mindoro. As yet, however, the main bulk of the dipterocarp forest remains untouched and large quantities of Tanguile, Red Lauan, and Apitong still await the lumberman.

The present methods of operation make it almost impossible to estimate the cost of logging accurately. Such an estimate, based on the best obtainable data, shows that the cost of delivering logs at the beach, at a distance of from 1 to 2 miles, ranges from ₱0.07 to ₱0.13 per English cubic foot. Counting an English cubic foot as equivalent to 7.2 feet B. M., this would be a cost of from ₱9.75 to ₱18 per 1,000 feet B. M. At present shipping facilities are very poor and transportation expensive, the latter being one of the largest items of expense. As there are no regular steamers which can be depended upon for this purposes,

---

[1] 2 pesos=1 dollar, United States currency.

large operators must provide their own transportation. Small cutters
ordinarily contract with sailing vessels to carry their timber to the
market. Sometimes they pay a fixed rate of from ₱0.20 to ₱0.30 per
cubic foot, while in other cases one-half of the selling price is given in
payment. A few men own small sailing ships.

At present there are four small sawmills in Mindoro, located at
Cauayan, Mangarin, Paluan, and Camarong. All of these are too light
to handle the heavy Philippine timbers and have proven unsatisfactory.
(Pl. X.) Nearly all of the lumber used locally is sawed by hand.

The main part of the timber output is sold at Manila, small shipments
going to Iloilo, Cebu, and other markets.[1]

The following market prices are those at present paid in Manila:

Manila market prices of lumber (Philippine currency.)

	Per 1,000 feet B. M.
Tanguile or Balacbacan	₱80–₱100
Apitong	70– 100
Lauan	60– 90
Guijo	98– 140
Malugay	95– 130
Molave	215– 300
Dungon	185– 200
Yellow Narra	225– 275
Red Narra	250– 300
Ipil	180– 225
Amuguis	110– 150
Palosapis	90
Calantas	180– 200
Tindalo	250– 300
Acle	280– 300
Yacal	170– 200
Balacat (Bigaa)	100
Palo Maria	140– 160

The forests of Mindoro to-day offer many inducements to the lumberman looking for opportunities for investment. To the large operator,
the dipterocarp forests are the most promising. Stands are heavy and
good grades of timber are secured, while the general topography of the
country is such as to permit the use of logging machinery. Those
without sufficient means to undertake the business upon a large scale in
a modern way can hardly hope to handle this grade of timber success-
fully. Small cutters will find abundant opportunity for logging in

---

[1] For more complete information concerning markets, etc., see Bulletin 4,
Bureau of Forestry, I. Mechanical Tests, Properties, and Uses of Thirty-four
Philippine Woods; II. Philippine Sawmills, Lumber Market and Prices; and
Circular No. 2, Bureau of Forestry, P. I. (1908).

the forests along the coast where much timber is still to be had within easy reach of the beach.   The slopes of the Pinamalayan Mountains, the flat-land forests of eastern Mindoro, and the forests around Mount Calavite are among the best available locations.

MINOR PRODUCTS.

FIREWOOD.

The Philippine market to-day requires about 180,000 cubic meters of firewood annually to meet its demands.   The larger proportion of this comes from the mangrove swamps, the woods of which are well adapted to that purpose.

One company is operating in the Baco River swamps and is keeping a large force of men at work continuously.   No other extensive swamp areas are located so close to Manila as are those of Mindoro, nor are there many locations where loading can be so well carried on during the southwest monsoon season, when Manila prices are highest, as in the Calapan and Pola Bays.

With the increase in development of the Philippines and the constant demand for firewood, a fairly constant market is assured to the near-by Mindoro product, and lumbermen operating in northeastern Mindoro districts will no doubt find this business a profitable adjunct to their main enterprise.

TANBARK.

At present a small amount of tanbark is gathered from the mangrove-swamp trees, almost all of which, as shown by analyses already given, contains a fair amount of tannic acid.   Good-sized areas and heavy stands of these trees are found in all mangrove-swamps.   These facts, in view of the growing shortage of tanning material in the United States and elsewhere, make it very likely that the manufacture of tannin extract, or "cutch," will be undertaken in the Philippines within a comparatively short time.

The mangrove-swamps lend themselves readily to management, reproducing well and growing rapidly, so that companies willing to undertake this enterprise in connection with the cutting of firewood, may be assured of a constant supply.

BEJUCO.

Bejuco (rattan) is gathered in small quantities at present.   Measurements of bejuco growing upon two plots, each 25 meters square, showed a yield at the rate of 12,000 meters of merchantable product per hectare. These two plots were taken at random in one of the best bejuco districts of the east forest and are an indication of what can be secured in the best situations.   Although good prices are paid for this product, no one has yet succeeded, nor in fact seriously attempted, to place it on the market in sufficient quantities to supply the demand.

OTHER PRODUCTS.

Almaciga, a valuable resin, is the product of the Almaciga tree, which occurs scattered quite generally over the mountains and ridges above 2,000 feet altitude, especially in the northwestern part of Mindoro. The resin is found in large deposits in the ground, where it has no doubt accumulated gradually through long periods. No estimates were made of the amount of this product available.

Brea (elemi), the gum of the Pili tree, is gathered in small quantities, and used locally for torches.

Dyebark, from the Nigue or Tabigue tree, is commonly gathered and sold, but is found in very limited quantities.

Although but little used in Mindoro, the leaves of the Buri palm may be made into hats, mats, baskets, etc. A good grade of sugar is made from its sap, which is also fermented and used as a beverage. The stem yields a starchy substance resembling sago. Large numbers of these valuable trees are found near the coast between Magaran and Mangarin, and between Uasig and Bongabon.

Nipa palm, the leaves of which are the commonest roofing material in the Philippines, abounds along the edges of the swamps.

Gogo (*Entada scandens* Benth.) is a vine, the stem of which is used by the natives as a soap for washing the hair. While common, it is gathered in limited quantities.

A score of other products might be mentioned, each of which is useful. Indeed, the forests are rich in their profusion of natural products and supply many of the wants of the inhabitants.

APPENDICES.

APPENDIX A.

STATISTICAL TABLES.

TABLE I.[a]—*Stand and estimated yield of trees over 40 centimeters (16 inches) in diameter in Narra.forest between the Dangay and Bongabon Rivers, eastern Mindoro.*

[Average of 28.39 hectares (70.15 acres.)]

Species.	Stand of trees—		Per cent.	Species.	Stand of trees—		Per cent.
	Per hectare.	Per acre.			Per hectare.	Per acre.	
Narra	4.77	1.98	7.16	Pili and Pagsahingin	1.05	.42	1.57
Lauan	14.81	5.99	22.23	Agupanga	4.71	1.91	7.07
Guijo	4.24	1.72	6.87	Malaicmo	3.12	1.27	4.69
Amuguis	4.70	1.90	7.06	Dao	3.40	1.37	5.10
Apitong	2.56	1.03	3.83	All others	21.50	8.70	32.26
Calumpit and other Terminalia spp	1.32	.54	1.98	Total	66.63	26.96	100
Hagachac	.45	.18	.68				

[a] For a detailed statement of this stand, as well as for that of the adjacent forest, see Merritt and Whitford: A Preliminary Working Plan for the Public Forest Tract of the Mindoro Lumber and Logging Company, Bongabon, Mindoro, P. I., Bur. of For. P. I., Bul. 6 (1906), p. 27.

Estimated yield in board feet per acre:

Narra	1,250	Calumpit		400
Lauan	6,850	Hagachac		280
Guijo	1,580			
Apitong	1,200	Total per acre		12,820
Amuguis	1,260	Total per hectare		31,670

TABLE II.—*Stand and estimated yield of trees, 30 centimeters (12 inches) and over in diameter, on Balete River flats, eastern Mindoro.*

[Average of 41.9 hectares (103.6 acres).]

Species.	Stand per hectare. [a]				Total per acre.	Per cent.
	Estimated diameter.					
	30–60 centimeters (1–2 feet).	60–90 centimeters (2–3 feet).	90 centimeters and over (3 feet and over).	Total.		
Lauan	6.65	4.70	2.88	14.23	5.76	11.80
Apitong	.45	.24	.17	.86	.35	.71
Dao	2.48	2.12	1.74	6.34	2.57	5.26
Calumpit and other Terminalia spp	1.09	.57	.36	2.02	.81	1.67
Malugay	1.95	1.36	.26	3.57	1.45	2.97
Amuguis	2.50	1.64	.42	4.56	1.85	3.79
Guijo	1.79	1.05	.71	3.55	1.44	2.95
Malaicmo	14.66	3.15	.17	17.98	7.27	14.90
Candol-candol	17.10	4.62	.62	22.34	9.04	18.52
Tanguile (Illipe ramiflora)	.31	.07	.02	.40	.16	.33
Agupanga	8.70	1.86	.19	10.75	4.35	8.91
Narra	.45	.24	.05	.74	.30	.61
All others	28.62	3.41	1.24	33.27	13.46	27.58
Total	86.75	25.03	8.83	120.61	48.81	100

[a] This table of stands, as in the case of all following, except as otherwise noted, was compiled from tree counts taken on regular strips through the forest. Distances were measured and diameters estimated.

Estimated yield [b] in board feet per acre:

Lauan	6,800
Apitong	400
Terminalia spp	500
Malugay	1,100
Amuguis	1,100
Guijo	1,600
Total per acre	11,500
Total per hectare	28,400

[b] This yield, as in the case of all following, unless otherwise stated, has been computed by applying such measurement of felled trees in Mindoro as are available to the stand tables given, and by comparing the forests with those of other regions where more detailed studies were made. Although estimates only, it has been the constant aim to make these statements conservative.

TABLE III.—*Stand and estimated yield of trees, 30 centimeters (12 inches) and over in diameter, on the low Quinibigan hills, eastern Mindoro.*

[Average of 15.6 hectares (38.5 acres).]

Species.	Stand per hectare.				Total per acre.	Per cent.
	Estimated diameter.					
	30–60 centimeters (1–2 feet).	60–90 centimeters (2–3 feet).	90 centimeters and over (3 feet and over).	Total.		
Lauan	3.40	4.81	3.08	11.29	4.57	8.48
Apitong	.83	.58	.45	1.86	.75	1.40
Dao	.64	.83	.39	1.86	.75	1.40
Calumpit and other Terminalia spp	.58	1.48	.64	2.70	1.09	2.02
Malugay	1.28	1.92	.77	3.97	1.61	2.99
Amuguis	.77	.64	.19	1.60	.65	1.20
Guijo	3.33	1.73	.70	5.76	2.33	4.34
Malaicmo	15.83	6.47	.45	22.75	9.21	17.12
Candol-candol	12.56	4.74	1.02	18.32	7.42	13.79
Tanguile (Illipe ramiflora)	.32	.06	.06	.44	.18	.34
Agupanga	3.40	2.18	.13	5.71	2.31	4.29
Narra	.26	.19	.06	.51	.21	.38
All others	41.28	11.80	3.08	56.16	22.73	42.24
Total	84.48	37.43	11.02	132.93	53.81	99.99

Estimated yield in board feet per acre:

Lauan	6,700
Apitong	900
Terminalia spp	1,000
Malugay	1,900
Amuguis	400
Guijo	2,100
Total per acre	13,000
Total per hectare	32,100

TABLE IV.[a]—*Stand and estimated yield of trees, 30 centimeters (12 inches) and over in diameter, on Pula River flats, northeastern Mindoro.*

[Average of 6.2 hectares (15.3 acres).]

Species.	Stand per hectare.				Total per acre.	Per cent.
	Estimated diameter.					
	30–60 centimeters (1–2 feet).	60–90 centimeters (2–3 feet).	90 centimeters and over (3 feet and over).	Total.		
Lauan	0.16	0.32	0.97	1.45	0.59	1.59
Tanguile (Illipe ramiflora)	.16	0.00	0.00	.16	.06	.18
Dao	.65	1.93	1.93	4.51	1.82	4.96
Calumpit and other Terminalia spp	.16	.65	.32	1.13	.46	1.24
Malugay	.16	.16	.16	.48	.19	.53
Amuguis	.97	1.61	.81	3.39	1.37	3.73
Guijo	.16	0.00	0.00	.16	.06	.18
Candol-candol	.64	.32	.48	1.44	.59	1.58
Agupanga	9.18	5.31	.32	14.81	6	16.28
Banaba	1.61	1.93	.32	3.86	1.56	4.24
Bolongeta	2.25	.48	0.00	2.73	1.11	3
Malaicmo	10.79	5.96	0.00	16.75	6.78	18.41
All others	25.12	12.24	2.74	40.10	16.23	44.08
Total	52.01	30.91	8.05	90.97	36.82	100

[a] Computed from counts made on a single line crossing the broad river flat east and west, east from Pinamalayan.

Estimated yield in board feet per acre:

Lauan	1,300
Terminalia spp	400
Malugay	300
Amuguis	1,200
Banaba	700
Total per acre	3,900
Total per hectare	9,600

TABLE V.—*Stand and estimated yield of trees, 30 centimeters (12 inches) and over in diameter, on south slope of Pinamalayan Mountains, northeastern Mindoro.*

[Average of 4.03 hectares (9.96 acres).]

Species.	Stand per hectare.				Total per acre.	Per cent.
	Estimated diameter.					
	30–60 centimeters. (1–2 feet).	60–90 centimeters. (2–3 feet).	90 centimeters and over. (3 feet and over).	Total.		
Malugay	4.7	5.2	2.2	12.1	4.8	23
Candol-candol	7.9	1.4		9.3	3.7	17.6
Amuguis	2.5	.5		3	1.2	5.7
Aglaia sp	2.5		.5	3	1.2	5.7
Malaicmo	2	.2		2.2	.9	4.2
Teluto	.7	.7	.2	1.6	.7	3
Lauan	.5	.7	.5	1.7	.7	3.2
Palaquium sp	1	.2		1.2	.5	2.3
Guijo	.5		.2	.7	.3	1.3
Dita	.5		.2	.7	.3	1.3
Bolongeta	.7			.7	.3	1.3
Pagsahingin	.5		.2	.7	.3	1.3
Banilad	.5		.2	.7	.3	1.3
Lanete	.5		.2	.7	.3	1.3
Narra			.5	.5	.2	1
Alupag	.5			.5	.2	1
Pili	.5			.5	.2	1
Ipil	.2			.2	.1	.4
All others	9.6	2.5	.6	12.7	5.1	24.1
Total	35.8	11.4	5.5	52.7	21.3	100

Estimated yield in board feet per acre:

Malugay	5,500
Amuguis	400
Lauan	1,000
Guijo	300
Narra	200
Total per acre	7,400
Total per hectare	18,200

TABLE VI.—*Stand and estimated yield of trees, 30 centimeters (12 inches) and over in diameter, on forest southwest of Lake Naujan, northeastern Mindoro.*

[Average of 41.65 hectares (102.9 acres).]

Species.	Stand per hectare.					Total per acre.	Per cent.
	Estimated diameter.				Total		
	30–60 centimeters (1–2 feet).	60–90 centimeters (2–3 feet).	90–120 centimeters (3–4 feet).	120 centimeters and over (4 feet and over).			
Alam	9	10.80	5.16	1.08	25.99	10.52	27.71
Lauan	4.49	8.60	.82	.24	9.15	3.70	9.75
Tanguile	1.61	1.90	1.95	.87	6.33	2.55	6.78
Apitong	1.47	1.25	.39	.02	3.18	1.26	3.32
Agupanga	3.89	.23	.17	---------	4.29	1.74	4.57
Malaicmo	1.18	.89	.02	---------	2.09	.84	2.22
Baticulin	.67	.05	---------	---------	.72	.29	.77
Palo Maria	.58	.26	.02	---------	.86	.35	.97
Calantas	.07	.07	.02	---------	.16	.07	.18
Amuguis	.19	.22	.02	---------	.43	.17	.46
Dao	.17	.05	.02	---------	.24	.10	.25
Guijo	.07	.02	---------	---------	.09	.04	.10
All others	30.52	9.27	.55	---------	40.34	16.32	42.98
Total	53.91	28.61	9.14	2.16	93.82	37.95	100.01

Estimated yield in board feet per acre:

Alam	14,800
Tanguile	5,700
Lauan	3,800
Apitong	1,500
Total per acre	25,800
Total per hectare	63,700

TABLE VII.—*Stand and estimated yield of trees, 30 centimeters (12 inches) and over in diameter, in the forest between the Binabay and Alag Rivers, northeastern Mindoro.*

[Average of 12.29 hectares (30.37 acres).]

Species.	Stand per hectare.					Total per acre.	Per cent.
	Estimated diameter.				Total.		
	30–60 centimeters (1–2 feet).	60–90 centimeters (2–3 feet).	90–120 centimeters (3–4 feet).	120 centimeters and over (4 feet and over).			
Tanguile	5.5	4.2	2.7	1	13.4	5.4	22.1
Alam	6	3.9	1.8	.2	11.9	3.8	19.7
Palosapis	3.2	2.7	1.5	.5	7.9	3.2	13
Apitong	7.9	3.5	.5	.2	12.1	4.9	19.9
Lauan	.5	.7	.2	---------	1.4	.6	2.4
All others	11.7	2	.2	---------	13.9	5.6	22.9
Total	34.8	17	6.9	1.9	60.6	24.5	100

Estimated yield in board feet per acre:

Tanguile	8,900
Alam	5,300
Palosapis	5,100
Apitong	4,300
Lauan	700
Total per acre	24,300
Total per hectare	60,000

TABLE VIII.—*Stand and estimated yield of trees, 30 centimeters (12 inches) and over in diameter, on the low hills east of the Ibolo River, north-central Mindoro.*

[Average of 1.66 hectares (4 acres).]

Species.	Stand per hectare.				Total per acre.	Per cent.
	Estimated diameter.					
	30–60 centimeters (1–2 feet.)	60–90 centimeters (2–3 feet).	90 centimeters and over (3 feet and over).	Total.		
Tanguile	7.4	8	5	20.4	8.2	33.4
Alam	8.7	3.7	.6	13	5.2	21.2
Lauan	1.8	.6		2.4	1	4
Apitong	1.2	.6		1.8	.8	3
All others	18.5	4.3	.6	23.4	9.5	38.4
Total	37.6	17.2	6.2	61	24.7	100

Estimated yield in board feet per acre:

Tanguile	12,600
Alam	3,700
Lauan	500
Apitong	500
Total per acre	17,300
Total per hectare	42,700

TABLE IX.[a]—*Stand and yield of trees, 25 centimeters (10 inches) and over in diameter, on Paluan River watershed, northwestern Mindoro.*

[Average of about 19.4 hectares (48 acres).]

Species.	Number of trees—		Per cent.	Species.	Number of trees—		Per cent.
	Per hectare.	Per acre.			Per hectare.	Per acre.	
Apitong	6.8	2.8	5.3	Malaruhat	3	1.2	2.3
Lauan	6	2.4	4.6	Amuguis	2	.8	1.5
Malugay	5.3	2.2	4.2	Molave	1	.4	.8
Guijo	5.2	2.1	4	Banaba	.4	.2	.4
Dungon	4.2	1.7	3.2	All others	87.7	35.5	67.7
Alupag	4.1	1.7	3.2				
Camagon	3.5	1.4	2.7	Total	129.2	52.4	99.9

[a] These stand tables and the estimates of yields which follow, were prepared by Foresters Hareford and Clark in 1902 by running valuation surveys in the regions named and calipering all trees over 25 centimeters (10 inches) in diameter. The yields were computed by applying the volume in cubic feet of the average tree, of those over 25 centimeters (10 inches) in diameter, to the stand tables given. The results have been changed to board feet, supposing that 1 cubic foot will cut 8 board feet. The yields thus obtained are slightly higher in proportion to the number of trees than have been given in previous tables.

Estimated yield in board feet per acre:

Alupag	500	Malugay	2,130
Amuguis	670	Molave	120
Camagon	400	Panao	1,890
Dungon	900		
Guijo	1,460	Total per acre	10,910
Lauan	2,840	Total per hectare	26,950

TABLE X.—*Stand and yield of trees, 25 centimeters (10 inches) and over in diameter, on Aloparis River watershed, northwestern Mindoro.*

[Average of about 1.8 hectares (4.75 acres).]

Species.	Number of trees—		Per cent.	Species.	Number of trees—		Per cent.
	Per hectare.	Per acre.			Per hectare.	Per acre.	
Uacatan	9.9	4	7.4	Dungon	2.3	.9	1.6
Malugay	6.8	2.8	5.1	Malaicmo	2.3	.9	1.6
Alacaac	5.3	2.2	4	Calamansanay	1.5	.6	1.1
Apitong	6	2.5	4.6	Calumpit	.7	.3	.6
Lauan	4.5	1.8	3.3	Malaruhat	.7	.3	.6
Camagon	4.5	1.8	3.3	All others	79.3	32.1	59
Alupag	3	1.2	2.2				
Duguan	3.8	1.5	2.8	Total	134.4	54.4	100
Guijo	3.8	1.5	2.8				

Estimated yield in board feet per acre :

Alupag	370		Lauan	2,740
Apitong (and Panao)	3,730		Malugay	3,850
Camagon	430			
Dungon	370		Total per acre	13,280
Guijo	1,790		Total per hectare	32,810

TABLE XI.—*Stand and yield of trees, 25 centimeters (10 inches) and over in diameter, on Calauagan River watershed, northwestern Mindoro.*

[Average of about 2.32 hectares (5.75 acres).]

Species.	Number of trees—		Per cent.	Species.	Number of trees—		Per cent.
	Per hectare.	Per acre.			Per hectare.	Per acre.	
Dungon	9.9	4	9.4	Malugay	2	.8	1.9
Lauan	6	2.4	5.7	Malaicmo	2	.8	1.9
Camagon	6	2.4	5.7	Molave	1.5	.6	1.4
Lanete	5	2	4.7	Calantas	1.5	.6	1.4
Calamansanay	3.5	1.4	3.3	Calumpit	1	.4	.9
Mambog	3	1.2	2.8	Batino	1	.4	.9
Uacatan	3	1.2	2.8	Ipil	.5	.2	.5
Alupag	3	1.2	2.8	All others	51.9	21	49.3
Banaba	2.5	1	2.3				
Teluto	2.5	1	2.3	Total	105.8	42.6	100

Estimated yield in board feet per acre :

Alupag	320		Malugay	2,130
Calamansanay	880		Molave	70
Camagon	560			
Dungon	4,020		Total per acre	10,770
Ipil	230		Total per hectare	26,610
Lauan	2,560			

TABLE XII.—*Stand and yield of trees, 25 centimeters (10 inches) and over in diameter, on Malugao River watershed, northwestern Mindoro.*

[Average of about 5.46 hectares (13.5 acres).]

Species.	Number of trees—		Per cent.	Species.	Number of trees—		Per cent.
	Per hectare.	Per acre.			Per hectare.	Per acre.	
Lauan	9.6	3.9	6.9	Camagon	2.5	1	1.8
Malugay	9.3	3.8	6.7	Apitong	2	.8	1.4
Dungon	8.4	3.4	6	Molave	1.7	.7	1.2
Bolongeta	6.2	2.5	4.4	Guijo	1.4	.6	1.1
Duguan	5.9	2.4	4.2	Ipil	.8	.3	.5
Alupag	5.6	2.3	4	All others	79.8	32.3	56.8
Calamansanay	3.7	1.5	2.6				
Amuguis	3.4	1.4	2.5	Total	140.3	56.9	100.1

Estimated yield in board feet per acre:

Alupag	1,070	Ipil	360
Amuguis	1,150	Lauan	4,150
Apitong	1,400	Malugay	3,740
Bolongeta	410	Molave	200
Calamansanay	1,060		
Camagon	340	Total per acre	18,270
Duñgon	2,340	Total per hectare	45,140
Guijo	2,050		

TABLE XIII.—*Stand and yield of trees, 25 centimeters (10 inches) and over in diameter, on Pametucan Mountain, northwestern Mindoro.*

[Average of about 1.2 hectares (3 acres).]

Species.	Number of trees—		Per cent.	Species.	Number of trees—		Per cent.
	Per hectare.	Per acre.			Per hectare.	Per acre.	
Lauan	16.5	6.7	8.3	Calamansanay	2.5	1	1.2
Narra	8.2	3.3	4.1	Dita	2.5	1	1.2
Malaicmo	8.2	3.3	4.1	Dao	3.3	1.3	1.6
Calumpit	7.4	3	3.7	Duñgon	1.6	.7	.9
Duguan	6.6	2.7	3.4	Molave	.8	.3	.4
Amuguis	5.8	2.3	2.9	Ipil	.8	.3	.4
Uacatan	5.8	2.3	2.9	All others	118.9	48.1	59.9
Abilo	5.8	2.3	2.9				
Malugay	4.1	1.7	2.1	Total	198.9	80.3	100

Estimated yield in board feet per acre:

Amuguis	2,060	Malugay	1,350
Calamansanay	520	Narra	2,770
Calumpit	4,400		
Duñgon	90	Total per acre	18,710
Ipil	400	Total per hectare	46,230
Lauan	7,120		

TABLE XIV.—*Stand and yield of trees, 25 centimeters (10 inches) and over in diameter, on north slopes of Calavite Mountain, northwestern Mindoro.*

[Average of about 13.35 hectares (33 acres).]

Species.	Number of trees—		Per cent.	Species.	Number of trees—		Per cent.
	Per hectare.	Per acre.			Per hectare.	Per acre.	
Manicnic (Uacatan and Mayusip)	11.1	4.5	7.1	Abilo	1.6	.6	1
Duguan	7.2	2.9	4.6	Duñgon	1.3	.5	.8
Malaruhat	5.2	2.1	3.3	Ipil	1.3	.5	.8
Malugay	4.7	1.9	3	Calantas	.4	.2	.3
Amuguis	4	1.6	2.5	All others	117.1	47.4	75.1
Bolongeta	2.2	.9	1.4	Total	156.1	63.1	99.9

Estimated yield in board feet per acre:

Amuguis	1,670	Manicnic (Mayusip and Uacatan)	1,730
Bolongeta	270	Narra	280
Calantas	520		
Duñgon	220	Total per acre	7,190
Ipil	220	Total per hectare	17,760
Malugay	2,280		

TABLE XV.—*Stand and yield of trees, 25 centimeters (10 inches) and over in diameter, on Agbanga River watershed, northwestern Mindoro.*

[Average of about 12.1 hectares (30 acres).]

Species.	Number of trees—		Per cent.	Species.	Number of trees—		Per cent.
	Per hectare.	Per acre.			Per hectare.	Per acre.	
Duguan	8.8	3.4	5.7	Tindalo	1.3	.5	.8
Malaruhat	6.3	2.5	4.2	Alupag	1.1	.5	.8
Malaicmo	3.1	1.3	2.2	Calamansanay	.7	.3	.5
Malugay	2.9	1.2	2	Lauan	.7	.3	.5
Amuguis	2	.8	1.3	All others	118.9	48.2	80.2
Abilo	1.6	.6	1				
Molave	1.3	.5	.8	Total	148.2	60.1	100

Estimated yield in board feet per acre:

Alupag	180	Molave	90
Amuguis	480	Tindalo	280
Calumpit	220		
Lauan	170	Total per acre	2,380
Malugay	960	Total per hectare	5,880

TABLE XVI.—*Stand and yield of trees, 25 centimeters (10 inches) and over in diameter, on Lemanao River watershed, northwestern Mindoro.*

[Average of about 6.88 hectares (17 acres).]

Species.	Number of trees—		Per cent.	Species.	Number of trees—		Per cent.
	Per hectare.	Per acre.			Per hectare.	Per acre.	
Molave	10.9	4.4	6.5	Camagon	2.5	1	1.5
Duguan	10.7	4.4	6.5	Bolongeta	2	.8	1.2
Malaruhat	9	3.6	5.3	Duñgon	2	.8	1.2
Amuguis	6	2.4	3.5	Alupag	1.4	.6	.9
Abilo	5.2	2.1	3.1	Calamansanay	.9	.4	.6
Malugay	3.7	1.5	2.2	Ipil	.7	.3	.4
Dao	3.7	1.5	2.2	Bansalaguin	.7	.3	.4
Acleng parang	3.4	1.4	2.1	All others	98.5	39.9	59.1
Uacatan	3.2	1.3	2				
Dita	2.6	1	1.5	Total	167.1	67.7	100.2

Estimated yield in board feet per acre:

Acleng parang	290	Ipil	240
Amuguis	1,970	Malugay	1,520
Bolongeta	200	Molave	700
Calumpit	200		
Camagon	190	Total per acre	5,640
Duñgon	300	Total per hectare	13,930

TABLE XVII.—*Stand and yield of trees, 25 centimeters (10 inches) and over in diameter, on Calansan River watershed, northwestern Mindoro.*

[Average of about 7.28 hectares (18 acres).]

Species.	Number of trees—		Per cent.	Species.	Number of trees—		Per cent.
	Per hectare.	Per acre.			Per hectare.	Per acre.	
Lauan	15.7	6.3	9.2	Amuguis	1	.4	.6
Calamansanay	7.1	2.9	4.3	Baticulin	1	.4	.6
Camagon	6.2	2.5	3.7	Narra	.8	.3	.4
Molave	4.4	1.8	2.6	Ipil	.7	.3	.4
Malaruhat	3.8	1.6	2.4	All others	124	50.2	73.6
Malaicmo	2.3	.9	1.3				
Alupag	1.5	.6	.9	Total	168.5	68.2	100

Estimated yield in board feet per acre:

Alupag	180	Molave	650
Amuguis	310	Narra	340
Calamansanay	1,280		
Camagon	580	Total per acre	9,570
Ipil	290	Total per hectare	23,640
Lauan	5,940		

TABLE XVIII.—*Stand of trees on an exceptionally heavy Parang near Maujao, Mindoro.*

[Average of 1.73 hectares (4.27 acres).]

Species.	Stand per hectare.				Total per acre.	Per cent.
	Estimated diameter.			Total.		
	10–30 centimeters (4 inches to 1 foot).	30–60 centimeters (1–2 feet).	60 centimeters and over (2 feet and over).			
Bancal	24.8	12.7	0.6	38.1	15.4	32.5
Putat	11	1.7		12.7	5.1	10.8
Banaba	13.3	1.7		15	6.1	12.8
Mambog	10.4	1.7		12.1	4.9	10.3
Tanog	6.3	1.2		7.5	3	6.4
Acleng parang	2.9	1.7	.6	5.2	2.1	4.5
Antidesma spp	3.5	.6		4.1	1.7	3.5
Cupang	1.1	.6		1.7	.7	1.4
Caña fistula	1.7			1.7	.7	1.4
Grewia tilaefolia	1.2			1.2	.5	1
Bombycidendron vidalianum		.6		.6	.2	.5
Narra	.6			.6	.2	.5
Cordia blancoi		.6		.6	.2	.5
All others	12.7	2.4	1.2	16.3	6.6	13.9
Total	89.5	25.5	2.4	117.4	47.4	100

TABLE XIX.—*Forest products which have been gathered from Mindoro, during the period from July 1, 1902, to June 30, 1908.*

Fiscal year.	Timber (cubic meters).	Firewood (cubic meters).	Tanbark[a] (quintals).	Dyebark[a] (quintals).	Bejuco[b] (pieces).
1902–3	3,708	2,462	406		97,649
1903–4	5,696	5,172			158,961
1904–5	6,983	6,510	3,502	187	777,838
1905–6	5,412	9,448	2,457	96	588,231
1906–7	8,610	4,902	2,902	409	836,080
1907–8	10,544	4,175	1,967	171	1,742,555
Total	[c]40,953	32,669	11,234	863	4,201,264

[a] Metric quintal of 220.46 pounds.
[b] Each piece of bejuco is usually about 6 meters long.
[c] One cubic meter of timber contains approximately 330 feet B. M. On this basis the entire amount of timber cut would be 13,514,490 feet B. M.

APPENDIX B.

In common with most tropical countries, the forests of Mindoro contain a great variety of tree species. Comparatively few of these are now or are ever likely to be utilized commercially. Only the important commercial species, with the most numerous or characteristic noncommercial kinds, have been mentioned in the preceding portion of the report. In order to give a more detailed idea of the composition of the forest, the following list of tree species has been added.

In addition to those collected by the writer, the list includes a number of other species from the following collectors; Mr. E. D. Merrill, botanist, Bureau of Science; Dr. H. N. Whitford, forester, Bureau of Forestry; Mr. T. E. Borden, collector, Bureau of Forestry; Mr. R. C. McGregor, ornithologist, Bureau of Science; and Mr. Robert Rosenbluth, forester, Bureau of Forestry. It includes practically all of the tree species which have been secured from Mindoro since the American occupation, but no doubt is far from complete.

The numbers following the scientific names are those upon the herbarium sheets in the Bureau of Science, and with the exception of the collections of Messrs. Merrill, Whitford, Borden, and McGregor, are of the regular Bureau of Forestry series. The other numbers are those of the collector in question.

Of the families represented, the *Dipterocarpaceæ* and *Leguminosæ* stand out preëminently as being the most important from a commercial standpoint. The "dipterocarps," as the members of the family *Dipterocarpaceæ* have well been called, are all large and tall-growing trees, most of them producing an excellent grade of general construction timber and some of them having wood which is well suited for cabinet purposes. This, together with the fact that they comprise a large part of the bulk of the timber in the forest, give them first place in order of commercial importance. The family *Leguminosæ* is easily of second rank. In this family are included Ipil, Narra, Tindalo, Acle, and Supa, woods which will probably compete with any other five of the world as beautiful and durable cabinet woods.

Several other families contain important commercial trees. The *Verbenaceæ*, of which family Teak (*Tectona grandis*) is a member, contain Molave and Sasalit, two woods which are hardly excelled for durability. It is also interesting to note that the many species of the genus *Eugenia* belong to the same family, the *Myrtaceæ*, as the Eucalypts of Australia. Some of these Eugenias are now and others are likely to be exploited commercially.

40

The writer is under obligation to Mr. E. D. Merrill, Dr. F. W. Foxworthy, and Dr. C. B. Robinson, botanists of the Bureau of Science, for making identifications of the specimens collected and to the first named for editing the following list of names.

The following abbreviations have been used in this list to indicate the sizes which the trees reach and the kind of situations in which they most commonly grow:

Sizes.—

A=Trees which are over 30 centimeters (12 inches) in diameter and more than 10 meters (33 feet) in height when mature.

B=Trees smaller than A, but more than 10 centimeters (4 inches) in diameter and more than 8 meters (26 feet) in height when mature.

C=Trees smaller than B.

Types of forest in which the trees most commonly occur.—

D=Dipterocarp forest.

V=Valley and coastal plain forest.

M=Dry-hill forest.

S=Mangrove swamps.

P=Parang.

H=High mountain tops and slopes.

B=Beach forest.

List of tree species collected in Mindoro and smaller adjacent islands.

[Families arranged according to the Engler and Prantl system.]

Species.	Size.	Type.	Common name.
TAXACEÆ.			
Dacrydium elatum (Roxb.) Wall., 4419	B	H	
Dacrydium falciforme (Parl.) Pilg., 4425		H	
Dacrydium sp., 8527	B	H	
Phyllocladus protractus (Warb.) Pilg., 5788 Merrill		H	
Podocarpus amarus Blume, 5703 Merrill		H	
Podocarpus blumei Endl , 5728 Merrill	B	H	
Podocarpus glaucus Foxw., 5672 Merrill		H	
Podocarpus imbricatus cumingii Pilg., 4446, 4471, 8528		H	Buyos.
Podocarpus neriifolius D. Don, 5768 Merrill	B	H	
Podocarpus pilgeri Foxw., 5754 Merrill		H	
Podocarpus rumphii Blume, 5553 Merrill	B	H	
Podocarpus sp., 11403, 6790	B	H	
PINACEÆ.			
Agathis philippinensis Warb., 8713, 11430	A	H	Almaciga.
Pinus merkusii Jungh., 8524, 8734 A., 8830, 8831	A	P H	Aguu.
PALMÆ.			
Areca catechu L., 12201 Rosenbluth		P	Bonga.
Areca whitfordii Becc., 1872 Whitford		V	Bongan-gubat.
Arenga mindoroensis Becc., 1790 Merrill		V	
Arenga saccharifera Labill., 4122		V	Irog.
Caryota sp., 1373 Whitford		V	Pugahan.
Cocos nucifera L.[1]			Coconut, Niog.
Corypha utan Lam., 4121		V	Buri.
Heterospatha elata Scheff., 9684		V	Sagasi.
Livistona mindorensis Becc., 4108		V	Anahao.
Orania pseudo-regalis Becc., 4120		V	Bonga.
Pinanga barnesii Becc., 9502		H	
Pinanga barnesii var. macrocarpa Becc., 6853, 11385		P H	
Pinanga elmeri Becc., 5555 Merrill		H	
Pinanga insignis Becc., 1388 Whitford		V	Sarauag.

[1] Not collected but commonly cultivated.

List of tree species collected in Mindoro and smaller adjacent islands—Continued.

Species.	Size.	Type.	Common name.
LILIACEÆ.			
Dracaena angustifolia Roxb., 9734	C	M	
CASUARINACEÆ.			
Casuarina equisetifolia Forst., 9739, 9740	A B	V H	Agoho.
Casuarina rumphiana Miq., 12029	B	H	Do
MYRICACEÆ.			
Myrica esculenta Buch.-Ham., 4433 Merrill	C	H	
Myrica javanica Blume, 5708 Merrill	C	H	
JUGLANDACEÆ.			
Engelhardtia spicata Blume, 5760 Merrill			
FAGACEÆ.			
Castanopsis philippinensis Vid., 8547	B	H	
Quercus soleriana Vid., 8586, 8721, 8749	A B	H	
Quercus sp., 9905, 11490, 12019	A B	H	
ULMACEÆ.			
Celtis philippinensis Blanco, 3763, 6786, 6847, 6873, 8566	A	V	Malaicmo.
Gironniera celtidifolia Gaud., 4320, 4325	C	V	
Trema amboinensis Bl., 1382 Whitford	B	V D P	Anabion.
MORACEÆ.			
Artocarpus communis Forst., 9686	A	V	Antipolo.
Artocarpus cumingiana Trec., 7141	A	V	Anubing.
Artocarpus nitida Trec., 9894	A	V D	Cubi.
Artocarpus odorata Blco., 9886	A	V	Antipolo.
Artocarpus woodii Merr., 5557 Merrill			
Artocarpus sp., 6763, 6783, 6814, 7146	A	V	
Ficus anomala Merr., 4082, 4086			
Ficus arayatensis Warb., 8573	A	V P	Balete.
Ficus balete Merr., 8535	A	B	Balete.
Ficus barnesii Merr., 3711, 8659	A B	V	Tibig.
Ficus benguetensis Merr., 232 McGregor			
Ficus benjamina L., 9693	A	V B	
Ficus clusiflora Miq., 3736			
Ficus forstenii Miq., 9686	A	V	Balete.
Ficus hauili Blco., 3733, 3761, 5352, 8725	A	V	Hauili.
Ficus indica L., 5479, 8695, 9897	A	V	
Ficus merrittii Merr., 6852, 11466, 11477	A	H	
Ficus mindoroensis Merr., 3625			
Ficus minahassae Miq., 3704, 9885	A	V	Hagimit.
Ficus nota (Blanco) Merr., 3618, 6852	A B	V	Tibig.
Ficus philippinensis Miq., 8520	B	H	
Ficus pisifera Wall., 6809			
Ficus pseudopalma Blco., 6174	B	V	Niog-niog.
Ficus rostrata Lam., 8534	C	V	
Ficus rubrovenia Merr., 4326, 5486, 6779, 8621	B	D	Tubuyog.
Ficus ruficaulis Merr., 2471 Borden			
Ficus variegata Blume, 9817	A	V	Tangisang bayauac.
Ficus spp., 3659, 4055, 8515, 8600, 8577, 8542, 8671, 8728, 8775, 9606, 9743, 9906, 11473, 11377	.		
Taxotrophis ilicifolia Vid., 5869, 5871, 9841, 9876	B	M	Cuyos-cuyos.
URTICACEÆ.			
Cypholophus macrocephalus Wedd., 11441	C	V	
Laportea luzonensis Warb., 11379	B C	V	
Laportea meyeniana Warb., 3708	B C	V	Lipa.
Laportea mindanaensis Warb., 8706	B C	V	Lipa.
Leucosyke capitellata Wedd., 3676, 3691, 3725, 6831	C	V	Hanlagasi.
Leucosyke hispidissima Miq., 11461	C	V	
Pipturus asper Wedd., 3723, 5362, 12023	B	V	Hinadung.
Streblus asper Lam., 9671, 9690	B	V	Calios.
Villebrunea frutescens Bl., 11462, 11880	C	V	
PROTEACEÆ.			
Helicia sp., 8723	B	H	
OLACACEÆ.			
ʼrombosia philippinensis (Baill.) Rolfe, 6190, 9898	A	V D	Camayuan or Tamayuan.

List of tree species collected in Mindoro and smaller adjacent islands—Continued.

Species.	Size.	Type.	Common name.
NYCTAGINACEÆ.			
Pisonia umbellata Seem., 8678, 3749, 4105	A	V	Anuling.
Pisonia sp., 8765			Calumpang.
MAGNOLIACEÆ.			
Drimys piperita Hook., 4383, 4407	C	H	
Illicium sp., 4411	C	H	
ANONACEÆ.			
Canangium odoratum Baill., 8670, 5586	A B	V P	Ilang-ilang.
Drepananthus philippinensis Merr., 6896	B	V	
Goniothalamus elmeri Merr., 3629, 4354, 8586	B	V	
Goniothalamus obtusifolius Merr., 2183 Borden			
Goniothalamus sp., 5505, 6812	B	V	
Mitrephora reflexa Merr., 8675	B	V	Lanotan.
Mitrephora merrillii C. B. Robinson, 3703, 6202	B	V	Do.
Orophea cumingiana Vid., 185 McGregor			
Orophea sp., 6797			
Oxymitra lagunensis Elm., 5629 Merrill			
Phaeanthus acuminatus Merr., 4321, 6154	C	V	
Phaeanthus ebracteolatus Merr., 5648 Merrill			
Polyalthia sp., 9911, 11413	B	V	
Unona clusiflora Merr., 8674	B	V	Do
Unona merrittii Merr., 3712	B	V	
Unona mindorensis Merr., 5568, 4060 Merrill	A B	V	
Xylopia dehiscens (Bloo.) Merr., 4064, 9697	A B	V	
MYRISTICACEÆ.			
Gymnacranthera paniculata Warb., 11494	A B	D	
Horsfieldia ardisiaefolia Warb., 3617	B		
Horsfieldia merrillii Warb., 3696, 6755, 6905, 8525, 9890, 9969	A	V	Duguan.
Horsfieldia sp., 11440			
Knema heterophylla Warb., 245 McGregor	A B		
Myristica guatteriifolia A. DC., 8585	A	D V	Do.
Myristica philippensis Lam., 3686	A	V	Do.
Myristica simiarum A. DC., 231 McGregor			
Myristica sp., 3663, 3698, 3730, 5884, 6884			
MONIMIACEÆ.			
Kibara ellipsoidea Merr., 4314			
Kibara sp., 4343	C		
Matthaea chartacea Merr., 167 McGregor			
LAURACEÆ.			
Actinodaphne philippinensis Merr., 3667	A	V	Bacan.
Cinnamomum sp., 6813	B	V D	
Cryptocarya acuminata Merr., 3673, 4342	A B	V	Malabacauan.
Cryptocarya lauriflora (Blanco) Merr., 8609			
Cryptocarya sp., 6742, 9891			
Dehaasia triandra Merr., 3751, 4091, 4104, 6210	A	V	Marang, Anagas or Baslayan
Endiandra coriacea Merr., 1408 Whitford	A		
Litsea garciae Vid., 6808, 6893	A	D V	Bangulo.
Litsea fulva F.-Vill., 6140	B C		
Litsea perrottetii F.-Vill., 3671. 6167, 6171	A	V	Bacan or Baticulin.
Litsea philippinensis Merr., 6161			
Litsea tersa Merr., 2158 Merrill	B	V	Ingas or Balanganan.
Litsea sp., 8545			
Litsea sp., 1413 Whitford			
Litsea sp., 4098	A B	V	Anagas.
Neolitsea vidalii Merr., 4092	A B		Lanutan puti.
Neolitsea villosa Merr., 4369, 8747			
Neolitsea sp., 8683, 11467	B	H	
Phoebe sterculioides (Elm.) Merr., 6859, 6824, 11381	A	D	Baticulin or Caboro.
HERNANDIACEÆ.			
Hernandia peltata Meisn., 5309			Calumpang.
CAPPARIDACEÆ.			
Crataeva religiosa L., 8815	B	P	
MORINGACEÆ.			
Moringa oleifera Lam., 925 Merrill			

List of tree species collected in Mindoro and smaller adjacent islands—Continued.

Species.	Size.	Type.	Common name.
SAXIFRAGACEÆ.			
Hydrangea lobbii Maxim., 5731 Merrill	C	H	
Polyosma philippinensis Merr., 8522	B	H P	
PITTOSPORACEÆ.			
Pittosporum odoratum Merr., 5654 Merrill	B C		
Pittosporum sp., 5392, 9845	B C	B	
CUNONIACEÆ.			
Weinmannia hutchinsonii Merr., 8782	B	H	
ROSACEÆ.			
Parinarium griffithianum Benth., 8639, 9708, 9711	A	V M	Liusin.
Pygeum glandulosum Merr., 3719, 6898, 12018	B	D	
Pygeum preslii Merr., 6744, 6784, 6854	B		
LEGUMINOSÆ.			
Acacia farnesiana Willd., 8564, 8834	C	P	Aroma.
Albizzia lebbekoides Benth., 9815	B	M	
Albizzia littoralis T. & B., 3685, 9678	A B	B V	Casay.
Albizzia procera Benth., 9704	A	P	Anapla or Acleng Parang.
Albizzia saponaria Bl., 11419	B	V P	
Caesalpinia sappan L., 9822	C	M	Sibucao.
Cassia fistula L, 8581	A	M	Caña fistula.
Cassia nodosa Ham., 9688	A	M	Do.
Cynometra simplicifolia Harms, 9908	A	D	
Desmodium umbellatum D C., 9675	B	B	
Erythrina indica Lam., 8770, 9695	A B	B	Dap-dap.
Gliricidia sepium (Jacq.) Steud., 8532	B	V	Cacauati or Madre Cacao.
Intsia acuminata Merr., 4119	A	V	Ipil.
Intsia bijuga O. Kuntz, 5373, 9877	A	V	Do.
Millettia merrillii Perk., 9821	B	M	
Pahudia rhomboidea Prain, 6735, 6739	A	M	Tindalo or Balayong.
Parkia roxburghii G. Don[1]	A	V	Cupang.
Peltophorum ferrugineum Benth., 9823	A	B	
Pithecolobium acle Vid., 9723	A	V	Acle.
Pithecolobium angulatum Benth., 3692, 4100, 5321	B	B	
Pithecolobium scutiferum (Blanco) Benth., 4073, 4099, 6211, 8570	A B	B	Anagap or Bansilac.
Pithecolobium prainianum Merr., 8508, 8719	B	H	
Pithecolobium sp., 6842			
Pongamia glabra Vent., 8645	B	B	
Pterocarpus echinatus Pers., 9895	A	H V	Narra.
Pterocarpus indicus Willd., 3675, 5876, 5881, 6721, 8655, 9744	A	V	Do.
Serianthes grandiflora Benth., 9735	A	B	
Sindora supa Merr., 9863	A	M	Supa.
OXALIDACEÆ.			
Averrhoa bilimbi Linn., 3642, 3722, 6184	C	V	Calamias or Iba.
RUTACEÆ.			
Atalantia disticha Merr., 6145, 5400	C	V D	
Citrus acida Roxb., 8835	C	V P	
Evodia latifolia DC., 3734, 4047, 8581, 12000	B	V	Cahoy dalaga.
Evodia reticulata Merr. 5711 Merrill	C		
Evodia retusa Merr., 8780	C	H	
Evodia triphylla DC., 6749	C	V D	
Fagara integrifolia Merr., 3659, 6169	A B	V	Silay.
Glycosmis cochinchinensis (Lour.) Pierre, 6722			
Lunasia amara Blco., 8572	B	V D	
Micromelum pubescens Bl., 8563	C	B	Peris.
Micromelum tephrocarpum Turcz., 3680			
Murraya exotica L., 4074 Merrill	C		Camuning.
Murraya sp., 6155	C	V	
SIMARUBACEÆ.			
Brucea mollis Wall., 12011	C	D	
Samadera indica L., 3738, 4061	B	V	Manungal.

[1] Not collected but very common.

List of tree species collected in Mindoro and smaller adjacent islands—Continued.

Species.	Size.	Type.	Common name.
BURSERACEÆ.			
Canarium carapifolium Perk., 2146 Borden			
Canarium gracile Engl., 3750, 4094	B	V	Sahing-sahing.
Canarium luzonicum A. Gray, 4062	A	V	Pili.
Canarium minutiflorum Engl., 6858	A	D	
Canarium perkinsae Merr., 3622, 3695, 11443	A B	V	
Canarium radlkoferi Perk., 3728, 3627, 9880	A B	V	Bugo.
Canarium stachyanthum Perk., 2177 Borden			
Canarium villosum Bl., 1378 Whitford	A	V	Pagsahingin.
Garuga abilo Merr., 8705	A	B M	Abilo, Bugo.
Santiria sp., 9831, 6781	A	D	
MELIACEÆ.			
Aglaia argentea Bl., 8662	B	L	
Aglaia denticulata Turcz., 3748	C		
Aglaia harmsiana Perk., 3638, 4095, 8702	B	V	Daranuras.
Aglaia luzoniensis M. &. R., 3623, 3661, 3677, 3745, 3756	A B	V	Calamismis.
Aglaia turczaninowii C. DC., 8569	A B	V	
Aglaia sp., 9810, 9888			
Aglaia sp., 9812	A B	M	Calantas.
Aphanomyxis sp., 8549	A	B	
Chisochiton philippinum Harms, 4037, 3679, 3729, 8785	A B		
Chisochiton sp., 6159, 3664			
Chisochiton tetrapetalus Harms, 4097			
Dysoxylum cauliflorum Hierns, 8672, 11481	B	V	
Dysoxylum decandrum (Blco.) Merr., 2140 Borden			
Dysoxylum pauciflorum Merr., 9727, 9837	A	M	Amas.
Dysoxylum rubrum Merr., 3735	C		
Dysoxylum turczaninowii A. DC., 9818	A	M V	
Dysoxylum sp., 3620, 9900			
Melia candollei Juss., 11384	A	D	Libas.
Reinwardtiodendron merrillii Perk., 6192, 9971	B	V	Bianti.
Sandoricum indicum Cav., 9717	A	V	Santol.
Sandoricum vidalii Merr., 6745	A	V	Malasantol.
Toona calantas, Merr., 8669, 9721	A	M V	Calantas.
Vavaea sp., 9811	A	M	
Xylocarpus granatum Koenig, 8571, 9864	A B	S	Piagao.
Xylocarpus obovatus Juss., 4033, 4035, 5316, 5425, 9791	A B	S	Nigue or Tabigue.
POLYGALACEÆ.			
Xanthophyllum sp., 7145, 8704, 8710	B		
DICHAPETALACEÆ.			
Dichapetalum monospermum Merr., 6807, 12009	B	D	
EUPHORBIACEÆ.			
Acalypha stipulacea Klotz., 11372, 8801, 6903	C	P	
Alchornea javensis (Bl.) Muell. Arg., 6719	B	V	
Antidesma bunius (L.) Spr., 9848, 9786	B	P	Bignay.
Antidesma edule Merr., 4051	B	P	Do.
Antidesma ghaesembilla Gaertn., 4072, 5312, 8820, 9703	A B	P	
Antidesma leptocladum Tul., 5513, 5717 Merrill	A B		
Antidesma sp., 5403, 6736	B	P	
Aporosa symplocosifolia Merr., 6764	B	D	
Baccaurea tetrandra Baill., 6734	B	D	
Bischofia trifoliata Hook., 5356, 5866, 9729	A	V	Toog.
Breynia cernua Muell. Arg., 262 McGregor	C		
Breynia acuminata Muell. Arg., 11432	C		
Claoxylon sp., 4332, 4329, 4364	C		
Cleistanthus myrianthus Kurz, 1812 Merrill	B C		Camandiis.
Cyclostemon bordenii Merr., 4067, 4068	B	V	Putian.
Cyclostemon microphyllus Merr., 4090, 6785, 9828	B	V	Butong-manoc.
Cyclostemon monospermus Merr., 5393	B		
Cyclostemon sp., 4084, 9733, 9909			Bato-bato.
Daphniphyllum glaucescens Blume, 5658 Merrill			
Endospermum peltatum Merr., 6891	A	V	Buluang.
Excoecaria agallocha L., 5420, 9846	B C	B	
Glochidion littorale Blume, 4115	C		
Glochidion philippicum (Cav.) Benth., 1393 Whitford, 4076, 9691	B	V	Uanguang.
Glochidion spp., 3645, 3744, 8781, 8852, 9803, 11431, 12031			
Homalanthus fastuosus F.-Vill., 5593 Merrill	B	P	
Homalanthus populneus Pax, 4452, 8812	B	H	
Homonoia riparia Lour., 247 McGregor	C	V	
Jatropha curcas L., 5365	C	P	Tuba.

List of tree species collected in Mindoro and smaller adjacent islands—Continued.

Species.	Size.	Type.	Common name.
EUPHORBIACEÆ—continued.			
Macaranga bicolor Muell. Arg., 8579, 12017	A B	V	Binunga.
Macaranga cumingii Muell. Arg., 9767			
Macaranga hispida Muell. Arg., 6899	B	V	Hamindang.
Macaranga mappa Muell. Arg., 6206	B	V	Binunga.
Macaranga tanarius Muell. Arg., 3706, 5810, 3742, 3762	A B	V	
Mallotus floribundus Muell. Arg., 3754, 11592, 11396	B		Tula-tula.
Mallotus moluccanus Muell. Arg., 3710, 6750, 12188	A B	V	Alim.
Mallotus muricatus Muell. Arg., 5874, 11451	B		
Mallotus philippinensis Muell. Arg., 9722	B		
Mallotus playfairii Hemsl., 4114			
Mallotus ricinoides Muell. Arg., 3631, 3709, 5422, 8592, 11463	B	V	
Mallotus sp., 5493, 6821			
Phyllanthus distichus Muell. Arg., 8612	C		
Sapium lateriflorum Merr., 9913			
Trewia ambigua Merr., 11369	A	V	
ANACARDIACEÆ.			
Buchanania arborescens Bl., 6168, 6769, 8821, 9710, 9814	A	V M	Balinhasay.
Buchanania nitida Engl., 4042	A	V	
Dracontomelum cumingianum Baill., 6189, 8757	A	V	Bagulibas.
Dracontomelum dao M. & R., 3683, 3684, 5476	A	V	
Koordersiodendron pinnatum Merr., 9723	A	V	Amuguis.
Mangifera altissima Blco., 9678, 9718	A	V	Pahutan.
Mangifera indica L., 985 Merrill	A	P	Mango.
Semecarpus elmeri Perk., 111 McGregor			
Semecarpus perrottetii glabra March., 928 Merrill	B	V P	Ligas.
Semecarpus philippinensis Engl., 11393	A B	V P	Do.
Semecarpus sideroxyloides Perk., 2160 Borden		V P	
Semecarpus spp., 8649, 8818, 9710, 9718, 9832	A B	V P	
Spondias mangifera Bl., 140 McGregor			
AQUIFOLIACEÆ.			
Ilex cymosa Bl., 11457	B	P	
Ilex fletcheri Merr., 4475, 4448	C H		
CELASTRACEÆ.			
Euonymus javanicus Blume, 6798			
Euonymus philippinensis Merr., 306 McGregor			
Kurrimia luzonica Vid., 6766	A B	D	
Lophopetalum toxicum Loher, 6805	A B	D	Dayandang.
Siphonodon celestrineum Griff. 4053	C	V	
STAPHYLEACEÆ.			
Turpinia pomifera DC., 8663, 8667	B C	V	Castanas.
ICACINACEÆ.			
Stemonurus cumingianus Miers, 11493	B	D	Barabo.
Stemonurus merrittii Merr., 9915, 9916	B	V D	
Urandra luzoniensis Merr., 6214	A	V	
SAPINDACEÆ.			
Allophylus ternatus Radlk., 5431, 5485	C		
Dodonaea viscosa L., 5397, 8851	C		
Erioglossum rubiginosum Bl., 9773, 9852	B	P	Tagoreron.
Euphoria cinerea Radlk., 3758, 9743, 9836	A	V D M	Alupag.
Guioa perrottetii Radlk., 8796, 9859	B	V	
Guioa pleuropteris Radlk., 12030	B	V	
Guioa sp., 8817	B C	P	Caninging.
Harpullia arborea (Blco.) Radlk., 8676, 8707	A B	V M	
Pometia pinnata Forst., 6133, 6800, 6801, 9713	A	V M	Malugay or Carunyan.
Tristira triptera Radlk., 9860	A B	P	
Tristira sp., 4063			Tagumtagum.
RHAMNACEÆ.			
Alphitonia excelsa Reiss., 11370, 5582 Merrill	B	D V	Dunglu.
Zizyphus inermis Merr., 9830	A	M	
Zizyphus mollis Merr., 8654, 9726	A	V M	Bigaa or Balacat.
Zizyphus zonulatus Blco., 6723	A	V	Do.
VITACEÆ.			
Leea aculeata Blume, 8751	C	V	
Leea sp., 5813	C	V	Calyautan.

List of tree species collected in Mindoro and smaller adjacent islands—Continued.

Species.	Size.	Type.	Common name.
ELAEOCARPACEÆ.			
Elaeocarpus argenteus Merr., 4462	B		
Elaeocarpus merrittii Merr., 4427			
Elaeocarpus multiflorus F.-Vill., 835 McGregor	B		
Elaeocarpus oblongus Gaertn., 3727	B	V	
Elaeocarpus pendulus Merr., 5727, 6204		H	
Elaeocarpus spp., 3674, 4387, 4409, 11482	A B	V	
GONYSTYLACEÆ.			
Gonystylus bancanus (Miq.) Gilg, 4098, 4344, 9839, 9899	A	V	
TILIACEÆ.			
Columbia subaequalis Planch., 9865	A B	P	Anilao.
Columbia serratifolia DC., 9772, 9995, 9865	A B	P	Do.
Diplodiscus paniculatus Turcz., 9840	A	M	
Grewia multiflora Juss., 3759, 5367, 8726	B	P	Bagocon.
Grewia stylocarpa Warb., 4085, 6836, 9903	A B	V	
Grewia tiliaefolia Vahl, 8799, 8824, 8652, 9709	B	P	Baronhasi.
Grewia umbellata Roxb., 8823	B	P	Basalon.
Halconia involucrata Merr., 5527 Merrill			
Trichospermum trivalve Merr., 1391 Whitford			
MALVACEÆ.			
Bombax ceiba L., 8763	A	B V	Babuy gubat.
Bombycidendron vidalianum M. & R., 9854	A B	P	
Ceiba pentandra L., 8531	A	V	Bulac, cotton tree or Copal.
Hibiscus tiliaceus L., 5324	B	B	Malibago.
Thespesia populnea (L.) Soland., 5421, 8540, 8578, 9698	B	B	Banago.
STERCULIACEÆ.			
Commerçonia platyphylla Andr., 3757, 5328	B		Culilio.
Heritiera littoralis Dry., 5483, 5391, 9677, 9679, 9779, 9719	A	V S	Dungon-late.
Kleinhofia hospita L. f., 9725	B	V	Tanag.
Pterocymbium tinctorium Merr., 2139 Borden	A	V	Teluto.
Pterospermum diversifolium Bl., 8601	B	V	Bayog.
Pterospermum niveum Vid., 8648, 8831, 9884	A B	V	Do.
Sterculia blancoi Rolfe, 4083, 5386	A	V	Candol-candol.
Sterculia crassiramea Merr., 8664, 8767	A		Banilad.
Sterculia cuneata R. Br., 3665, 5376, 9738	B	V P	Salimbubu.
Sterculia foetida L., 8764	A	V B	Calumpang.
Sterculia graciliflora Perk., 3646	A B	V	
Sterculia oblongata R. Br., 9879	A	V	Banilad.
Sterculia philippinensis Merr., 4052, 8683	A	D V	Do.
Sterculia stipularis R. Br.,			
Sterculia sp., 8541			
Tarrietia sylvatica Merr., 8576, 8574, 8761, 8651, 8603, 8829	A	M	Dungon.
Theobroma cacao L., 11395	C B	V P	Cacao.
DILLENIACEÆ.			
Dillenia philippinensis Rolfe, 9687, 6902, 9883	A B	V	Catmon.
Dillenia speciosa (Presl) Gilg, 11391	A B	V	Do.
Saurauia elegans (Choisy) F.-Vill., 5655			
Saurauia latibracteata Choisy, 5690, 5528 Merrill			
Saurauia philippinensis Merr., 4394			
Saurauia subglabra Merr., 8643	A B	M	
THEACEÆ.			
Adinandra sp., 4410, 4453, 8720, 4344	B C	H	Puyaca.
Eurya acuminata Wall. var. euprista Dyer, 5749, 6146 Merrill			
Eurya japonica Thunb., 11434, 4431	C	H	
Eurya sp., 4448, 6768	C	H	
Gordonia sp., 9757	A	H	
Ternstroemia sp., 4478			
Thea sp., 4328	C	D	
GUTTIFERÆ.			
Calophyllum blancoi P. & T. 12242 Rosenbluth			
Calophyllum cumingii P. & T., 8826	A	D H	Bantoogan or Bitanhol.
Calophyllum inophyllum L., 5395, 9696	A	B	Palo maria de la playa.
Calophyllum whitfordii Merr., 6855	A	D H	Palo maria.
Cratoxylon floribundum F.-Vill., 4071, 11390	B	V D	Cancilay or Guyon-guyong.
Cratoxylon sp., 12006	B	V	
Garcinia eugeniaefolia Wall., 11398, 6762, 6767, 6818, 11487	A B	D	Basan.

List of tree species collected in Mindoro and smaller adjacent islands—Continued.

Species.	Size.	Type.	Common name.
GUTTIFERÆ—continued.			
Garcinia rubra Merr., 3657, 4322, 8776	B	V	Camandiis.
Garcinia venulosa Choisy, 1802 Merrill	B		
Kayea paniculata Merr., 3747, 4056	B	V	
DIPTEROCARPACEÆ.			
Anisoptera thurifera Bl., 11401, 11408, 11389	A	D	Mayapis.
Dipterocarpus affinis Brandis, 1404, 1477 Whitford	A	D V	Hagachac.
Dipterocarpus grandiflorus Bl., 6160, 8802	A	D	Apitong.
Dipterocarpus hasselti Bl., 6811	A	D	Do.
Dipterocarpus vernicifluus Bl.,4101, 4106, 5475	A	D V	Apitong or Panao.
Hopea acuminata Merr., 7147	A	D	Mangachapuy or Dalindingan.
Hopea plagata Vid., 12028	A	D	Maliuin or Yacal.
Hopea (?) sp., 11399, 8742, 12027, 6726	A	D	Sarabsaban or Yacal.
Pentacme contorta M. & R. 8682, 9910, 4480, 12012	A	D V	Lauan.
Shorea guiso Bl., 9712, 8673, 8783, 12025, 5387, 11887, 8778, 9766, 8587	A	D V	Guijo.
Shorea polita Vid., 9806	A	D V	Lauan.
Shorea polysperma Merr., 8628, 11407, 12010, 12018, 12026, 11402, 6791, 6826, 11410, 8780	A	D	Balagayan, Bacnitan or Tanguile.
Shorea squamata Dyer, 6799, 8743, 6806, 11386, 6823, 11400	A	D	Alam, Tabac, or Red Lauan.
FLACOURTIACEÆ.			
Casearia fuliginosa Blco., 11496	B	V	
Casearia solida Merr., 8650	B	V	
Casearia sp., 5402			
Flacourtia sepiaria Clos, 9736	C	P	Bolong.
Flacourtia sp., 5413			
DATISCACEÆ.			
Octomeles sumatrana Miq., 4054	A	V	Binuang.
THYMELÆACEÆ.			
Phaleria cumingiana F.-Vill., 3632	C		
Wikstroemia viridifolia Meisn., 3320 Merrill			
LYTHRACEÆ.			
Duabanga moluccana Bl., 9818, 11409, 11435, 12079	A	V	Loctob.
Lagerstroemia speciosa (L.) Pers., 6822, 8652, 9705	A	V P	Banaba.
Pemphis acidula Forst., 932 Merrill			
SONNERATIACEÆ.			
Sonneratia pagatpat Blco., 4034, 5418, 9788	A	S	Pagatpat.
LECYTHIDACEÆ.			
Barringtonia luzoniensis Rolfe, 3746, 8624	B	V H	Putat.
Barringtonia racemosa Bl., 3640, 5499, 5571, 9699	A B	V	Do.
Barringtonia reticulata Miq., 3639, 4041, 5325, 5377, 6829	B	V	Do.
Barringtonia speciosa Forst., 5487	B	B	Botong.
RHIZOPHORACEÆ.			
Bruguiera caryophylloides Bl., 7137, 9825	A'B	S	
Bruguiera eriopetala W. & A., 5315, 9782	A B	S	Pototan.
Bruguiera gymnorrhiza Lam., 5414, 9138	A'B	S	Busiin.
Bruguiera parviflora W. & A , 5424, 5416, 7139, 8543, 9781	A B	S	Jangaray.
Carallia integerrima DC., 8840, 9896, 11366	A	V	Magua.
Ceriops candolleana Arn., 5415, 9816, 9850, 9851, 9795, 9790	A B	S	Tangal.
Gynotroches axillaris Blume, 4323			
Rhizophora conjugata L., 7140, 9779, 9780	A	S	Bacauan.
Rhizophora mucronata L., 5318, 9783	A	S	Do.
COMBRETACEÆ.			
Lumnitzera littorea (Jack) Voigt, 5427, 9807, 9892	B	S	Culasi.
Terminalia catappa L., 9694	A B	V B	Talisay.
Terminalia edulis Blco., 7142, 8848	A	V	Calumpit.
Terminalia ellipsoidea Merr., 11888	A	V D	Talisay gubat.
Terminalia multiflora Merr., 6193, 8708	A	M	
Terminalia nitens Presl, 7148	A	V	Sacat.
Terminalia pellucida Presl, 3699	A	V	Malagabi.
Terminalia sp., 9882	A	V	Calumpit.

List of tree species collected in Mindoro and smaller adjacent islands—Continued.

Species.	Size.	Type.	Common name.
MYRTACEÆ.			
Eugenia bataanensis Merr., 8687, 8734			
Eugenia bordenii Merr., 3700, 8841	A		Malaruhat or Macaasin.
Eugenia cinnamomea Vid., 9847	B		
Eugenia gigantifolia Merr., 4110, 5428, 4359	A	V	Malatalisay.
Eugenia javanica Lam., 4040, 5384, 9700, 9728	A	V	Malaruhat.
Eugenia luzoniensis Merr., 9781			Macupa.
Eugenia malaccensis L., 4065			
Eugenia mananquil Blanco, 3658, 6143, 11428	C	V	Bua-bua.
Eugenia merrittiana C. B. Robinson, 9751, 9920			
Eugenia mimica Merr., 8849			
Eugenia xanthophylla C. B. Robinson, 9875			Tampuy.
Eugenia spp., 8548, 8663, 6767, 8709, 9820, 5409, 4367, 4353, 5430, 6818, 6762, 8661, 8709, 8827, 8847, 8734, 9853			
Leptospermum flavescens Sm., 8526, 8523			
Mearnsia halconensis Merr., 5792 Merrill			
Psidium guajava L., 2166 Borden		P	Bayabas or guava.
MELASTOMATACEÆ.			
Astronia cumingiana Rolfe, 9765	B	H	
Astronia meyeri Merr., 4347	C	H	
Astronia sp., 6817			
Melastoma fuscum Merr., 9902	C	H D	
Melastoma polyanthum Bl., 6758, 8832	C		
Memecylon cumingianum Presl, 5323, 5432, 8634	B C		
Memecylon edule Roxb., 5509	C	D	
Memecylon preslianum Triana, 8658	B		Guis-guis.
ARALIACEÆ.			
Aralia glauca Merr., 6177 Merrill			
Aralia hypoleuca Presl [1]			
Arthrophyllum sp., 6181, 8627	B C	V	
Boerlagiodendron sp., 8750	C	H	
CORNACEÆ.			
Alangium meyeri Merr., 3643, 3682, 6136	A B	V	Putian.
CLETHRACEÆ.			
Clethra lancifolia Turcz., 8729	C	H	
Clethra williamsii C. B. Robinson, 4755	C	H	
ERICACEÆ.			
Diplycosia merrittii Merr., 4413, 4415, 4437	C	H	
Rhododendron quadrasianum Vid., 4408, 6158, 4455	C	H	
Vaccinium benguetense Vid., 12083	A	H D	
Vaccinium halconense Merr., 4422	B	H	
Vaccinium barandanum Vid., 5524 Merrill	C	H	
MYRSINACEÆ.			
Aegiceras corniculatum Blanco, 5317, 5419	B	S	
Ardisia boissieri DC., 4355, 4371, 8509	B	H	
Ardisia elmeri Mez, 4441, 4457			
Ardisia humilis Vahl, 3636, 5514, 11456	B C	P H	
Ardisia perrottetiana A. DC., 6215	C	V	
Ardisia racemoso-paniculata Mez, 4334			
Ardisia serrata (Cav.) Pers., 4372, 11012	C	H	
Ardisia serrata (Cav.) Pers. var. brevipetiolata Merr., 4346			
Ardisia sp., 6804, 6835	C		
Discocalyx cybianthoides Mez, 8656	B	M	
Embelia halconensis Merr., 5771 Merrill	B C	H	
Rapanea philippinensis Mez, 5481, 5515			Gaod-gaod.
Rapanea retusa Merr., 4426, 4449, 5734, 5735 Merrill	C	H	
SAPOTACEÆ.			
Chrysophyllum roxburghii Don, 9907	C	D	
Illipe ramiflora Merr., 5354	A	V	Tanguile.
Mimusops elengi L., 6781, 9701, 9702, 8759	A	B M	Bansalaguin.
Palaquium cuneatum Vid., 9866	A		
Palaquium gigantifolium Merr., 6787	A		
Palaquium lanceolatum Blco., 8714, 8730	A		Yangawan, Malac-malac, or Nato.
Palaquium latifolium Blco., 950 Merrill	A		

[1] Not collected but reported by E. D. Merrill as occurring commonly.

List of tree species collected in Mindoro and smaller adjacent islands—Continued.

Species.	Size.	Type.	Common name.
SAPOTACEÆ—continued.			
Palaquium luzoniense Vid., 3689, 4038, 6788, 7144, 9901	A	V	Malac-malac or Nato.
Palaquium oleiferum Blco., 9688, 9715	A	M	Alacaac, Malac-malac, or Nato.
Palaquium tenuipetiolatum Merr., 8599, 8701	A	M	Mayusip, Malac-malac, or Nato.
Palaquium sp., 6782, 6788, 9764			
Sideroxylon ferrugineum H. & A., 9673	A	V	
Sideroxylon macranthum Merr., 9833, 9835, 8670	A	M	
Sideroxylon stenophyllum Merr., 8626	A		
EBENACEÆ.			
Diospyros canomoi A. DC., 226 McGregor			
Diospyros discolor Willd., 8668	A B	M	Camagong.
Diospyros maritima Blume, 9834, 9899	B	M	
Diospyros nitida Merr., 9784	A B	M	Carnung.
Diospyros pilosanthera Blco., 5389	A B	V M	Bolongeta.
Diospyros sp., 5405, 5426			
Maba buxifolia Pers., 8828, 9661	B	M	Ebony.
SYMPLOCACEÆ.			
Symplocos adenophylla Wall., 4406, 4428, 4440			
Symplocos ferruginea Roxb., 8590	C	H	
Symplocos sp., 4447	C	H	
OLEACEÆ.			
Linociera cumingiana Vid., 9692	A B	M	
Linociera sp., 8700, 8703	A B	M	Alicatgang or Dayandang.
LOGANIACEÆ.			
Couthovia celebica Koord., 3697			Salinuoc.
Ligustrum cumingianum Vid., 9868	B	M	
Fagraea fragrans Roxb., 8842	A B	V	Susulin.
Fagraea morindæfolia Bl., 5480			
APOCYNACEÆ.			
Alstonia macrophylla Wall., 4067, 7149	A B	V	Batino.
Alstonia scholaris R. Br., 9720	A	D V	Dita.
Cerbera odollam Gaertn., 8544	B	B	
Kickxia merrittii Merr., 11488	A B	H D	Ayete.
Rauwolfia amsonisæfolia A. DC., 9792, 9855			Sibacon.
Tabernæmontana pandacaqui Poir., 5388	C	V P	
Tabernæmontana sp., 6743	C	V P	
Voacanga globosa (Blco.) Merr., 4075	B	V	Alibotbot.
Wrightia laniti (Blco.) Merr., 5378, 5380, 9801	A B	M P	Lanete.
BORRAGINACEÆ.			
Cordia blancoi Vid., 9862, 9793, 9856, 9849	A B	B P	Anonang.
Cordia subcordata Lam., 5507	B		
Tournefortia argentea L. f., 8554, 6733	A B	B	
VERBENACEÆ.			
Avicennia officinalis L., 9796, 9808	B	S	Api-api.
Callicarpa blancoi Rolfe, 4077	C	V P	Tigao.
Callicarpa caudata Maxim., 5556			
Callicarpa erioclona Schauer, 4078	C	V P	
Callicarpa formosana Rolfe, 3705, 5441	C	V P	Do.
Callicarpa sp., 4077	C	V P	
Clerodendron macrostegium Schauer, 3707	C	V P	Bangac.
Clerodendron simile Merr., 4043	C	V	
Clerodendron sp., 728	C	V	
Gmelina villosa Bl., 4080, 4079, 9798	C	P	Talungan.
Premna integrifolia L. f., 5401, 5492, 8538	B	V	Alagao.
Premna subglabra Merr., 12024	B	V	
Vitex aherniana Merr., 12236 Rosenbluth			Sasalit.
Vitex littoralis Decne., 8660, 8561, 8771	A	M P	Molave.
Vitex pubescens Vahl, 9800	A	M P	Do.
Vitex turczaninowii Merr., 9716, 9912	A	V D	Molauing aso.
BIGNONIACEÆ.			
Dolichandrone spathacea K. Sch., 5327, 9789	B	B V	Tuiy.
Radermachera mindorensis Merr., 2240, 2473 Merrill	A	V M	Banay-banay.
Radermachera pinnata Seem., 9717	A	V M	Do

List of tree species collected in Mindoro and smaller adjacent islands—Continued.

Species.	Size.	Type.	Common name.
RUBIACEÆ.			
Chasalia curviflora Thw., 3662 _____			
Gardenia barnesii Merr., 6144 _____	C	V	
Guettarda speciosa L., 8539, 9676 _____	B C	V	Tabon-tabon.
Hedyotis elmeri Merr., 4381 _____			
Ixora coccinea L., 11453 _____	C	V	
Ixora macrophylla Bartl., 3715, 8641 _____	C	V	Amuyong gubat or Tagpo.
Ixora sp., 5355, 8657 _____			
Lasianthus copelandi Elmer, 5778 Merrill _____			
Lasianthus lucidus Blume, 3325 Merrill _____			
Lasianthus obliquinervis Merr., 6189 Merrill _____			
Lasianthus stipularis Bl., 4077 _____			
Lasianthus tashiroi Matsum., 5739, 5776 Merrill _____			
Mitragyne diversifolia Hook., 8582, 9707 _____	A B	P	Mambog.
Morinda bracteata Roxb., 3718, 3760 _____			Nino.
Morinda citrifolia L., 5414 _____			Taing-aso.
Mussaenda anisophylla Vidal, 4330, 8779 _____	C	V P	Agboy.
Mussaenda frondosa L., 4049 _____	C	V P	Do.
Mussaenda grandiflora Rolfe, 3732 _____	C	V P	Do.
Nauclea bartlingii DC., 3694, 4088, 11459 _____	B	V	Hambibalad.
Nauclea gracilis Vid., 11412 _____	A B	D	
Nauclea media Hav., 8665 _____	A B	V M	Bano.
Nauclea reticulata Hav., 12014 _____	A B	V	
Nauclea sp., 4337, 8610, 8760 _____	A B	M	Bagurilao, or Calaman-sanay.
Pavetta dolichostyla Merr., 3714 _____	C	V	
Plectronia sp., 4059 _____			Liung-liung.
Psychotria luzoniensis F.-Vill., 8597, 8844, 9869 _____	B	M	Altoco.
Psychotria manillensis Bartl., 312 McGregor _____			
Psychotria sp., 4324, 4365, 4349, 9926 _____			
Randia mindoroensis Elmer, 3326 Merrill _____			
Sarcocephalus cordatus Miq., 4070, 9706 _____	A	V P	Bancal.
Sarcocephalus sp., 8533 _____	A	V	Do.
Stylocoryne macrophylla Bartl., 3726 _____	A	V	Basa.
Timonius appendiculatus Merr., 9867 _____	B		
Urophyllum bataanense Elm., 4339, 4348 _____	C	V	
Wendlandia luzoniensis DC., 6759, 8838, 8845 _____	B	P	

CPSIA information can be obtained
at www.ICGtesting.com
Printed in the USA
LVHW091839091219
639936LV00012B/416/P